# AI Prompt Engineering

## ABSOLUTE BEGINNER'S GUIDE

No experience necessary!

Michael Miller

P"

# AI Prompt Engineering Absolute Beginner's Guide

ISBN-13: 978-0-13-557046-3
ISBN-10: 0-13-557046-8

Library of Congress Control Number is on file.

1 2025

## Trademarks

**Head of Enterprise Content and Training, Enterprise Learning and Skills**
Julie Phifer

**Executive Editor**
Laura Norman

**Acquisitions Editor**
Anshul Sharma

**Marketing**
Rosa Wan

**Development Editor**
Charlotte Kughen

**Managing Editor**
Sandra Schroeder

**Senior Project Editor**
Mandie Frank

**Copy Editor**
The Wordsmithery LLC

**Designer**
Chuti Prasertsith

**Indexer**
Cheryl Lenser

**Proofreader**
Rick Kughen

**Compositor**
Bronkella Publishing LLC

**Graphics Processing**
tj graham art

# Contents at a Glance

# Table of Contents

# About the Author

This book is written by me, **Michael Miller**. Having written one best-selling book (*Using Artificial Intelligence: Absolute Beginner's Guide*), a training course, and numerous articles about artificial intelligence, I am apparently an AI expert—at least on the end-user level. (I don't pretend to be a developer in any way, shape, or form.)

Equally important, I've written more than 200 books over the past four decades, including the aforementioned one about AI and several others in the *Absolute Beginner's Guide* series. My readers say I have a knack for explaining complex technologies in easy-to-understand terms, and who's to argue with what my readers think? My books have collectively sold more than 2 million copies worldwide, which I'm justifiably proud of.

I have always had an interest in new and evolving technologies. I've been around long enough to experience and write about many different "new" technologies, from the original IBM PC in the 1980s to the Internet in the '90s to social media in the 2000s. AI is just the next new technology to explore.

Now a bit about me. I reside in a suburb of Minnesota's Twin Cities and do almost all my writing in a handful of local coffeeshops. (I drink chai, not coffee, however.) In addition to writing books like this one, I play drums, hang out with my eight grandkids, and write about music from the '60s, '70s, and '80s in my *Classic Song of the Day* blog (www.classicsongoftheday.com). I also have a YouTube channel you might want to check out, at www.youtube.com/@MichaelMillerWriter; there's some interesting and educational stuff there.

If you want to find out more about me and what I'm up to, check out my website, located at www.millerwriter.com. Feel free to use the contact form there to get in touch with me. I'm interested in all that anybody might have to say or ask, even though may not always be able to respond personally. I appreciate any feedback you might have.

# Dedication

*To my grandkids, in chronological order: Collin, Alethia, Hayley, Judah, Lael, Jackson, Jamie, and Addie. They're growing up in a much different world than the one I knew when I was their ages.*

# Acknowledgments

Thanks to the crew at Pearson for suggesting and helping to shepherd this book to conclusion, including but not limited to Laura Norman, Anshul Sharma, Mandie Frank, Rick Kughen, and Charlotte Kughen.

# We Want to Hear from You!

As the reader of this book, *you* are our most important critic and commentator. We value your opinion and want to know what we're doing right, what we could do better, what areas you'd like to see us publish in, and any other words of wisdom you're willing to pass our way.

We welcome your comments. You can email or write to let us know what you did or didn't like about this book—as well as what we can do to make our books better.

*Please note that we cannot help you with technical problems related to the topic of this book.*

When you email, please be sure to include this book's title and author as well as your name and email address. We will carefully review your comments and share them with the author and editors who worked on the book.

Email: community@informit.com

# Reader Services

Visit our website and register this book at informit.com/register for convenient access to any updates, downloads, or errata that might be available for this book.

# Figure Credits

This title includes images generated by the author using the following AI tools:

Adobe Firefly

BetterPrompt

ChatGPT

Claude (Anthropic)

Craiyon

DeepSeek

Dreamstudio by Stability AI

God of Prompt

Google Gemini

MetaAI

Microsoft Bing Image Creator

Midjourney

Mureka

OpenArt

Suno

Udio

# Introduction

So, you want to become more proficient in your use of artificial intelligence (AI) tools. That is presumably why you're now reading this book. Good for you; hopefully I'll provide you with the information and skills you need to become a proficient AI prompt engineer.

When it comes to AI, which is a topic none of us seems to be able to avoid, I am of mixed minds. I see its value but also see its limitations. Let me elaborate.

First, the obvious. AI is a really big deal and is going to get even bigger. There's no question that AI will have a significant impact on many professions. Because it can quickly recognize patterns in vast amounts of data, AI stands to revolutionize scientific and medical research, as well as automate a lot of currently manual tasks. We will go further and faster with AI's help.

Then there's the impact of AI on business. If AI isn't impacting your job yet, it will—soon and perhaps in a major way. Many, many employers are looking to use AI to take over certain business functions, which will improve their profits while at the same time cause untold numbers of people to lose their jobs. On the other hand, if you manage to keep your job through the AI revolution, you'll probably be able to use artificial intelligence tools to become more efficient in it. So, there's that.

AI also looks to revolutionize our personal lives. AI tools will help you make better personal decisions, communicate better with others, and make more efficient use of your time. Over time, you may come to think of AI as an indispensable part of your life.

All that said, AI is not perfect—nor is it the be-all, end-all for all of society's ills. AI is only as good as the data it trains on, and that data comes from us human beings and our flawed human experiences. Because of that, it's quite possible that AI agents will only ever be average performers, not exceptional ones.

That's why I tend to think of artificial intelligence the same way I think of the Cliff character on the old *Cheers* television show. (If you're too young to remember *Cheers*, look it up online; it's probably streaming somewhere.) In that show, Cliff was the guy at the end of the bar who professed to be an expert on everything. Ask a question, and Cliff had an answer. ("Here's a little-known fact …")

The problem with Cliff was that he *didn't* know everything. While ol' Cliffie was a self-professed expert on every conceivable topic, he really didn't know as much as he thought. Cliff's knowledge, as the old saying goes, was a mile wide and an inch deep. He knew a little bit about a lot of stuff but not a lot about any given thing.

Worse, what Cliff didn't know, he made up. His proclamations might start out with a nugget of factual information but then veer off into wild speculation—speculation, one might recall, presented with an unerring air of authority.

It's the same thing with AI. AI doesn't know everything—and what it doesn't know, it makes up. Now, today's advanced AI models might be more knowledgeable than Cliff (and better guessers, too), but they still make up a lot of stuff a lot of the time. (When AI makes something up out of whole cloth, it's called a *hallucination*.) That's not good.

What I'm getting at is that while AI is important and will become more so, it's not perfect. You can, however, help AI achieve its highest potential by how you interact with it. That's what prompt engineering is all about.

# What Prompt Engineering Is—and What It Isn't

The phrase "prompt engineering" might be new to you. It certainly sounds very technical and impressive—scary, even.

Fortunately, prompt engineering isn't that technical or complex. It's just another way of saying "crafting effective prompts." As you probably know, a prompt is the input you provide to an AI model, and you craft a prompt pretty much the same way you craft a query to a web search engine. Nothing overly technical involved.

The big difference with an AI prompt, however, is that you need more than a word or two to get your point across. The more explicit your prompt—the more detailed and exact your instructions—the better the results you'll receive. That's what prompt engineering is all about: learning how to craft the most effective prompts possible.

What you might not know, or at least not yet, is that there are several different strategies you can employ when creating a prompt. Proper prompt engineering involves choosing the best prompt strategy, including all the necessary elements, and then fine-tuning your input until you get the output you want. It doesn't matter whether you're using AI to draft an email, create a presentation, or generate an image, the quality and completeness of your prompt will make all the difference in the world.

That's why I wrote this book—to help you become a better prompt engineer and get better AI results.

# What's in This Book

*AI Prompt Engineering: Absolute Beginner's Guide* is your guide to crafting more effective AI prompts. This book will take you through the figurative A to Z of prompt engineering, no prior experience required. I assume that you know a little bit about some of the most popular AI tools and that you've probably used some of these tools to some extent. You're not an AI expert, by any means, but you're at least familiar with the technology.

Let's be clear. While you're familiar enough with AI to know how to use it, you don't need to be an expert or an AI professional to use this book or to practice proper prompt engineering. This book is for the average user just dabbling in AI, as well as for more advanced users who need to use AI in their professions. It's a reality that users of all types and levels need to use prompt engineering to get better AI results, and this book is for everybody.

For that reason, *AI Prompt Engineering: Absolute Beginner's Guide* starts pretty much at the beginning, with a brief review of AI basics and an overview of today's most popular AI tools. From there, you'll delve right into the topics of prompt engineering—what it is, how it works, and how to use it. You'll discover the six major prompting strategies and when to use them, as well as how to employ prompt engineering for various AI-related tasks. You'll even get some predesigned prompt templates you can use in specific situations.

You start the book knowing little to nothing about prompt engineering and finish it being able to use prompt engineering to produce better AI results. That's time well spent, don't you think?

# How This Book Is Organized

The information in *AI Prompt Engineering: Absolute Beginner's Guide* is organized into 23 fairly accessible chapters plus one appendix. Here's how that information is presented:

**Chapter 1, "Understanding Generative AI":** A basic overview of today's artificial intelligence technology and a quick look at the most popular AI tools.

**Chapter 2, "What Is Prompt Engineering—and Why Is It Important?":** This is where you learn all about prompt engineering—what it is, how it works, and how to use it. It's all about the importance of proper prompt design.

**Chapter 3, "The Anatomy of a Perfect Prompt":** This chapter shows you the important elements of a prompt, how to structure an effective prompt, and what to include and not include in a prompt.

**Chapter 4, "Defining Output in Your Prompts":** This is a chapter about output format and style, and how to ensure that you get the right type of output you want.

**Chapter 5, "Understanding and Comparing Different Prompting Strategies":** Introducing the six essential prompt strategies and when to use each.

**Chapter 6, "Using Zero-Shot Prompting":** Zero-shot prompting is creating a prompt without providing any examples. Learn how and when to use this strategy.

**Chapter 7, "Using One-Shot Prompting":** This chapter introduces one-shot prompting, the strategy that involves creating a prompt that includes an example of the type and style of output you want.

**Chapter 8, "Using Few-Shot Prompting":** If one-shot prompting is good, few-shot prompting ought to be better, right? Find out in this chapter where you learn what few-shot prompting is, how to use it, and when it makes sense.

**Chapter 9, "Using Role-Based Prompting":** Sometimes you get better results by assigning AI a role or persona to shape its tone and style. This chapter will tell you all about it.

**Chapter 10, "Using Chain-of-Thought Prompting":** In this chapter, you learn how to create prompts that encourage AI to think step-by-step to reach a solution—and to display all the steps.

**Chapter 11, "Using Self-Consistency Prompting":** This one's all about asking the AI model to generate multiple reasoning paths and then select the most consistent results.

**Chapter 12, "Using Prompt Chaining":** This chapter is about a technique that uses multiple prompts linked together in a sequence to achieve the desired output.

**Chapter 13, "Using Multimodal Prompts":** Here's where you learn how to use multimodal prompts—prompts that, in addition to the traditional text prompt, utilize other types of input, such as text documents, images, and videos.

**Chapter 14, "Evaluating Prompt Performance":** How do you know when a prompt is working? This chapter is all about defining the metrics of success, using both quantitative and qualitative evaluation models.

**Chapter 15, "Refining Your Prompts":** Sometimes the AI doesn't get it right the first time. This chapter shows how to improve your results by using iterative prompting—and asking the AI to critique its own response.

**Chapter 16, "Prompting for Writing":** Now we get into how to use prompt engineering for specific types of tasks. In this chapter, we tackle prompt engineering for writing of all types, from social media posts and emails to research papers and novels.

**Chapter 17, "Prompting for Productivity":** In this chapter, you learn specific prompting techniques for different productivity use cases—business, education, medicine, and the like.

**Chapter 18, "Prompting for Image Generation":** Using AI to generate images is a whole other ball game, and this chapter details how to engineer your prompts for the types of pictures and drawings you want.

**Chapter 19, "Prompting for Video Generation":** If you thought prompting AI for image generation was different, wait till you learn how to use prompt engineering to create AI-generated videos—which is what this chapter is about.

**Chapter 20, "Prompting for Music Generation":** This chapter teaches you how to use prompt engineering to create your own AI-generated music.

**Chapter 21, "Advanced Prompting Strategies and Tools":** Learn even more tips and tricks for improving your prompts. Really.

**Chapter 22, "Prompting Responsibly":** This chapter is all about the ethical issues related to the use of AI, and how you can make sure you use AI ethically, responsibly, and legally.

**Chapter 23, "Troubleshooting Less-Effective Prompts":** Find out how to recognize and improve prompts that aren't quite right yet.

**Chapter 24, "Future Directions in AI and Prompt Engineering":** This final chapter wraps things up by discussing what's next for artificial intelligence technology and the art of prompt engineering.

In addition, there's an appendix after Chapter 24 that includes dozens of prompt templates for all types of AI-related tasks. If you're not sure what kind of prompt to create, that's the place to look.

One last thing. As you read through this book, you'll see a variety of notes that provide additional information—some of which is cautionary. You'll also find some extended sidebars that provide tangential information that might be interesting but not necessarily necessary. You may find them interesting or helpful.

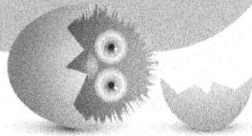

1

# UNDERSTANDING GENERATIVE AI

Generative artificial intelligence (AI) is changing the way we work and live our lives. Some experts think that AI is the biggest technological development of our lifetimes, or perhaps forever. AI is already being used by hundreds of millions of people worldwide and will become even more widely used in the months and years to come. But what exactly is artificial intelligence—and how does it work? Read on to find out.

# What AI Is

Let's start with the basics. What exactly is artificial intelligence?

Put simply, artificial intelligence is intelligence not naturally born. It's a simulation of natural human intelligence but created by machines.

AI is the providence of computer systems. It's all about computers that don't just compute but also "think." That means they don't merely regurgitate facts from existing sources but actually come up with new ideas and processes derived from existing material. AI "learns" from data to which it's been exposed, creating something new—just like human beings do.

The goal of AI is to create machines that not only can think like humans but also perform tasks that go beyond the capabilities of human minds. The technology works by ingesting and analyzing large amounts of data, identifying patterns, and extrapolating from those patterns to deduce solutions and make decisions.

**NOTE**    Know that AI isn't what some might call a "smart" application like one on your phone or computer. It's much more advanced than that. While some seek to exploit the buzz around AI by applying the term *artificial intelligence* to existing processes and applications, true AI goes well beyond those technologies we've been using for the past decade or so.

# How AI Works

Artificial intelligence is a complex technology that requires immense computing power and resources. It's more than just a simple computer program; it's a process that uses a variety of programs, algorithms, and technologies to achieve its results.

The AI process starts by collecting large amounts of data—articles, research papers, blog posts, images, videos, you name it. This data can come from a variety of sources. The AI engine needs this data as source material to learn how the world works, just as we humans need books and videos to feed us information.

With all this data in hand, the AI engine starts examining the data. It uses a variety of algorithms and technologies to extract key information from the assembled data, identify patterns, and make connections between different pieces of data.

Making these connections helps the AI model learn. It uses what it learned to make predictions, then evaluates its results and learns from them. It adapts based on these outcomes, essentially teaching itself from its experiences. Again, it's very much like the way we humans learn by experiencing and adapting, just all done by machine.

The AI learning process encompasses five distinct steps, as shown in Figure 1.1.

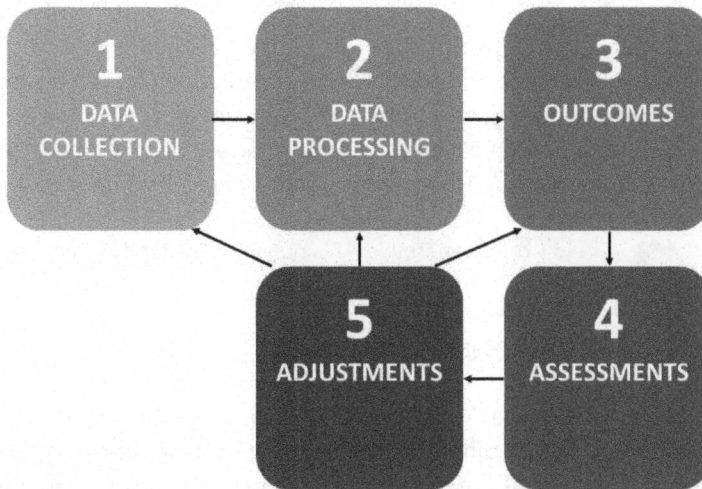

**FIGURE 1.1**

*The five steps of the AI process.*

1. **Data collection**, where the AI model assembles a vast amount of data of various types from a variety of sources.

2. **Data processing**, where the collected data is cleaned, processed, and analyzed using sophisticated *machine learning* (ML) algorithms, deep learning techniques, and *large language models* (LLMs); the goal is to identify patterns within the data.

3. **Outcomes**, where the identified patterns within the data are used to predict future outcomes; these outcomes are then compared to previous patterns to see if they match.

4. **Assessments**, where the predicted outcomes are assessed to gain further insight.

5. **Adjustments**, where data assessments are fed back into the process so that the model can make necessary adjustments to ensure better future outcomes.

In essence, the entire AI process is a giant feedback loop. As outcomes are assessed, the necessary adjustments are fed back into the data collection, data processing, and outcome steps to fine-tune the entire model. Thus, the AI model learns over time as it processes more and more data.

# How Generative AI Differs from Predictive AI

There are actually two types of AI in use today, predictive AI and generative AI. Predictive AI is focused on making specific predictions based on existing data, while generative AI can generate new content similar to and based on that existing data. Generative AI can generate text, images, videos, music, and other content that is often indistinguishable from that created by humans.

**NOTE**   Generative AI is not the ultimate form of artificial intelligence. This ultimate AI is called *artificial superintelligence*, and it's a future form of AI that surpasses human intelligence. We're not there yet.

Predictive and generative AI are related in that they use similar learning techniques, but substantially different in terms of what they're designed to achieve. In essence, predictive AI predicts future outcomes, whereas generative AI creates new outcomes. Predictive AI is smart, but generative AI is creative. Both have their place in our collective future.

Not surprisingly, generative AI models require larger datasets than predictive models. They also require a corresponding larger amount of computing power. (This is why predictive AI was developed first, while generative AI had to wait for more and more powerful technological resources to become practical.)

Table 1.1 details the differences between predictive AI and generative AI.

**TABLE 1.1**   Comparing Predictive AI and Generative AI

|  | **Predictive AI** | **Generative AI** |
|---|---|---|
| Objective | Predict future outcomes or trends | Generate new data or content |
| Data requirements | Historical and current data within a specific topic area | Large quantities of high-quality data |
| Output | Predictions based on input data | Newly generated text, images, videos, music, etc. |
| Applications | Finance, healthcare, marketing, chatbots, web search | Art and design, writing, music production, training simulations, application coding |
| Tech requirements | Moderate to high levels of computational power and data storage capacity | Much higher computational power and large data storage capacity |

Predictive AI has been in use in one form or another for some time. Generative AI is newer and the type of AI that everyone is excited about today.

# How People and Businesses Use AI

As you can imagine, AI is going to be an important technology for lots of people and businesses going forward. But what does it matter to you, personally?

There are many ways that individuals and businesses can use AI technology for their work and personal lives. In particular, you can use AI to

- Analyze complex scientific data
- Answer questions
- Automate business processes
- Automate manufacturing processes
- Create and manage legal contracts
- Create artwork and other images
- Create marketing plans and materials, including highly personalized advertisements
- Create music
- Create outlines
- Create personalized fitness plans
- Create realistic gaming environments and characters
- Create lesson plans for teachers
- Create travel plans and itineraries
- Create lifelike videos
- Diagnose medical conditions
- Evaluate loan risk
- Generate recipes and grocery lists
- Help with homework
- Manage inventory levels
- Power self-driving vehicles
- Provide customer support

- Provide financial advice

- Provide ideas for stories and other items

- Provide medical advice

- Research topics

- Summarize business meetings

- Talk with (as a digital assistant)

- Write letters and social media posts

- Write news stories and articles

- Write programming code

- Write school and business reports

That seems like a lot, but it's just scratching the surface of what AI can do. Bottom line, AI is going to be almost everywhere and do almost everything. AI will affect your life in ways you can't even imagine—both for better and for worse. That's why you need to know how AI works to get the most out of AI, using proven prompt engineering strategies, so you can better use it proactively in your own life.

# Today's Most Popular AI Tools

Whatever you want to use AI for, you have to employ an AI tool. Fortunately for you, today, there are numerous AI tools available for both personal and professional use. You just have to choose the right tool for your particular needs.

Some of these AI tools are free to use—at least for a limited number of prompts or a limited amount of time. Others require a subscription of some sort. Some offer affordable monthly subscriptions for consumers, and some offer more pricey subscriptions for businesses and professional users.

Many AI tools are general in nature, kind of all-purpose tools that can be used to generate all types of output. Other tools specialize in specific types of output, such as images, videos, or music. Some all-purpose tools can also generate images and the like; some can't.

With all that in mind, Table 1.2 details some of the most popular AI tools today and what you can use them for.

**TABLE 1.2**  Popular Generative AI Tools

| AI Tool | URL | Text | Images | Video | Music |
|---|---|---|---|---|---|
| Adobe Firefly | www.adobe.com/firefly/ | | Y | Y | |
| AIVA | www.aiva.ai | | | | Y |
| Artlist | www.artlist.io | | | Y | |
| Beatoven | www.beatoven.ai | | | | Y |
| Boomy | www.boomy.com | | | | Y |
| Canva AI | www.canva.com/ai-image-generator/ | | Y | | |
| ChatGPT | www.chatgpt.com | Y | Y | | |
| Choruz | www.choruz.ai | | | | Y |
| Claude | www.claude.ai | Y | | | |
| Deep Dream Generator | www.deepdreamgenerator.com | | Y | | |
| DeepAI | www.deepai.org | | Y | Y | Y |
| DeepSeek | www.deepseek.com | Y | | | |
| DreamStudio by Stability AI | www.dreamstudio.ai | | Y | | |
| Google Flow | labs.google/flow/about | | | Y | |
| Google Gemini | gemini.google.com | Y | Y | Y | |
| Grok | www.grok.com | Y | Y | Y | |
| Hailou AI | hailuoai.video | | Y | Y | |
| Hotpot | www.hotpot.ai | | Y | | |
| Jasper | www.jasper.ai | Y | | | |
| Kling AI | www.klingai.com | | | Y | |
| Luma Dream Machine | www.lumalabs.ai/dream-machine | | | Y | |
| Loudly | www.loudly.com | | | | Y |
| Meta AI | www.meta.ai | Y | Y | Y | |
| Microsoft Bing Image Creator | www.bing.com/images/create | | Y | | |
| Microsoft Copilot | copilot.microsoft.com | Y | | | |
| Midjourney | www.midjourney.com | | Y | Y | |
| Mureka | www.mureka.com | | | | Y |
| NightCafe | creator.nightcafe.studio | | Y | | |
| OpenArt | www.openart.ai | | Y | | |
| Perplexity | www.perplexity.ai | Y | | | |
| Paperpal | www.paperpal.com | Y | | | |
| Pi | www.pi.ai | Y | | | |
| Poe | www.poe.com | Y | | | |

| AI Tool | URL | Text | Images | Video | Music |
|---------|-----|------|--------|-------|-------|
| RiffGen | www.riffgen.com | | | | Y |
| Riffusion | www.riffusion.com | | | | Y |
| Runway | www.runwayml.com | | | Y | |
| Rytr | www.rytr.me | Y | | | |
| Sora | www.openai.com/sora/ | | Y | Y | |
| Soundful | www.soundful.com | | | | Y |
| Soundraw | www.soundraw.io | | | | Y |
| Sudowrite | www.sudowrite.com | Y | | | |
| Suno | www.suno.com | | | | Y |
| Udio | www.udio.com | | | | Y |
| Vidu | www.vidu.com | | | Y | |

With all these AI tools available (and more coming online seemingly daily), how do you choose which one to use?

While each of these tools is trained on a slightly different data set and each employs slightly different algorithms, they all work in pretty much the same fashion and provide similar but not identical results. While you won't get the same results from each tool, the individual results will all probably be acceptable.

Is any one of these tools significantly better than the others? In my experience, I'd have to say that I don't think so; the results are all acceptable yet different, just as you'd get different pieces of advice if you asked a handful of your friends the same question.

That said, you may find that you like the results (or how they're presented) from one tool better than the others. If so, that is probably the right tool for you. It comes down to being a personal choice.

The best thing to do is give them all a try. Prompt each one with a similar request and see what results you get. You can then choose the one that feels right to you—or use multiple tools as you prefer.

**NOTE**    Among the all-purpose generative AI tools, ChatGPT is arguably the most popular at the moment. Parent company OpenAI claims that ChatGPT has more than 180 million monthly users and that 80 percent of Fortune 500 companies have integrated ChatGPT into their operations. If you're only going to use one AI tool, ChatGPT is probably the place to start.

# How to Use an AI Tool

Almost all of these AI tools work in a similar manner. After you sign up or log in, you enter a prompt into the tool's prompt box, like the one shown in Figure 1.2. Be as descriptive as necessary when constructing your prompt. Press Enter when you're ready and let the tool do its thing. It's as simple and as complex as that.

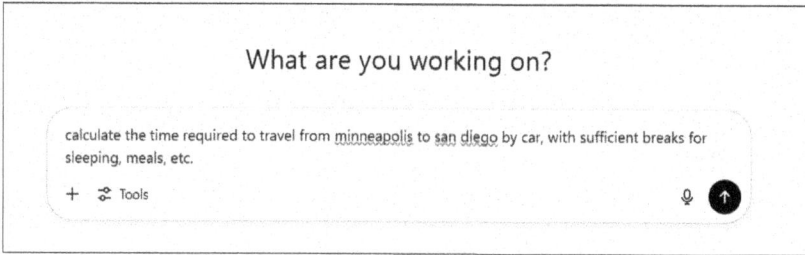

### What are you working on?

calculate the time required to travel from minneapolis to san diego by car, with sufficient breaks for sleeping, meals, etc.

+   ⇄ Tools                                    🎤   ⬆

**FIGURE 1.2**

*A typical prompt entered into the ChatGPT prompt box.*

Some AI tools offer additional options or controls. For example, an AI image generator, like the one in Figure 1.3, might let you choose what type of output you want (dimensions, art style, etc.), which you'd do by selecting the appropriate boxes or options. Others let you upload files to use as guidance or to analyze. Use the available options to help guide the tool to the output you desire (see Figure 1.3).

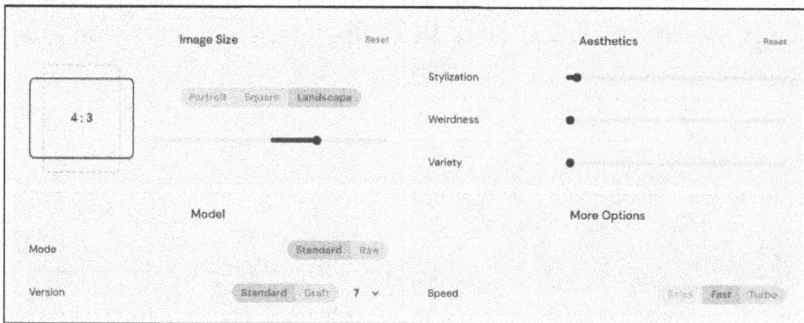

**FIGURE 1.3**

*Additional options available with the Midjourney image generator.*

The results you receive depend on what tool you're using and what you're trying to create. An all-purpose tool, such as Google Gemini or Meta AI, will present its results in a text stream that looks a lot like the messaging app on your smartphone. You can then enter additional prompts to continue a "conversation" with the AI tool (see Figure 1.4).

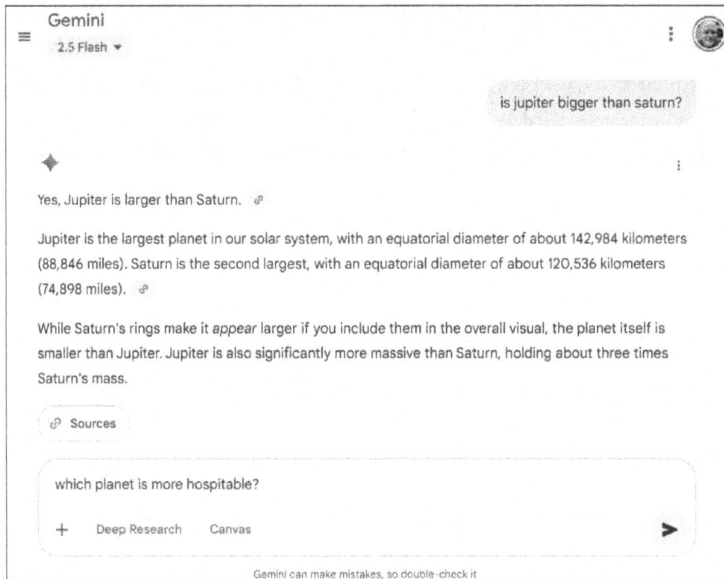

**FIGURE 1.4**

*An ongoing conversation in Google Gemini.*

AI image generators, of course, will present one or more images based on the information in your prompt, as shown in Figure 1.5. Video generators will present a video based on your input, and music generators will give you a song that sounds like what you requested. The output depends entirely on what you're creating.

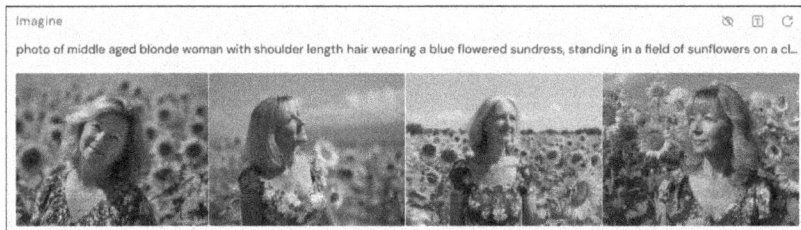

**FIGURE 1.5**

*Multiple images created from a Midjourney prompt.*

Just remember, you don't have to accept the first results you receive. You can rerun a prompt, either as-is or with fine-tuning, to generate additional results. As you'll learn throughout this book, the more detailed your prompts, the more you'll like the results.

# Summary

In this chapter, you found out what artificial intelligence is and how it works. You learned the difference between predictive AI and generative AI and the kinds of things for which you can use an AI tool. Finally, you discovered some of the most popular AI tools today and how to use them, in general.

Now it's time to learn more about creating the perfect AI prompt. Turn the page to Chapter 2 to learn more about prompt engineering!

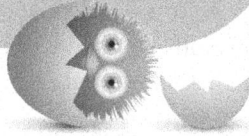

2

# WHAT IS PROMPT ENGINEERING—AND WHY IS IT IMPORTANT?

Prompt engineering is the key to making artificial intelligence useful in your daily life. Without prompt engineering, AI is nothing more than an amusing toy. With prompt engineering, AI becomes a useful tool with a wide variety of applications.

# What Is Prompt Engineering?

Prompt engineering is a fancy phrase for crafting effective prompts for use with AI models. It's both an art and a science that's necessary for getting the most out of today's AI tools.

In the world of artificial intelligence, a prompt is the input you provide to an AI model. It's how you communicate with AI, the instructions you provide that tell the AI model what you want it to do.

An AI prompt can take many forms. A prompt can be a question, a command, or a description of what you want. A prompt can be a complete sentence or paragraph or just a few words in an incomplete sentence. It can be a set of detailed instructions or just a general suggestion. You can use proper grammar and punctuation or not; periods and question marks are not required.

In short, a prompt is whatever is necessary to convey to an AI tool what it is you want. Think of it as asking a friend to do something for you. It's as simple and as complex as that.

Prompt engineering is how you approach crafting an AI prompt. While you can enter a "freeform" prompt into an AI prompt box, that isn't prompt engineering. Prompt engineering requires more thought and planning—and produces better results.

It's the difference between setting out on a drive with only a general sense of where you want to go versus planning your trip with maps and a detailed set of driving instructions. Prompt engineering is a planned trip that gets you where you want to go in the most efficient fashion.

# What Does Prompt Engineering Entail?

As noted, a prompt is just a set of instructions you give to an AI model, whether that's for answering a question, generating a post or an article, or creating an image or video. To get the results you want, you need to provide extremely clear instructions to whichever AI model you're using. That means constructing prompts that include all the information that the AI model needs to generate the desired output.

I go into more detail about how to create AI prompts in Chapter 3, "The Anatomy of a Perfect Prompt," but in general, you need to do the following:

- Choose the right words; be as descriptive as possible.

- Provide the proper context and details; don't leave anything to chance.

- Specify the output format; the AI model needs to know what it is you want to create.

- Specify a tone or style.

- Provide examples, if necessary.

Think of an effective AI prompt like a set of instructions you might give to someone doing a job for you. The more detailed your instructions, the easier it is for that person to perform the work the way you want it. It's the same thing with artificial intelligence; effective prompt engineering requires you to include all the elements necessary for AI to generate the output you expect.

# Why Is Proper Prompt Design Important?

It's important that you provide an AI model the most detailed, precise prompt you can muster. Just tossing off a short prompt without a lot of specifics will generate results that *might* be what you were looking for, but more likely not. You need to engineer your prompts in such a way that the AI model knows exactly what you want. There are a number of reasons for this.

## Random Prompts Give You Random Results

You know how to enter a search query into Google, so you should be able to craft a decent AI prompt, right? Just type a few words to describe what you want and let the AI model do its thing.

Unfortunately, it isn't that easy. Working with AI is trickier than working with a simple web search engine. If you enter a random prompt, you're going to get random results.

Why is working with AI so difficult? It's because AI models don't understand the world the way that you and I do. AI neither grasps the nuances of language nor has real-world experiences to draw upon. AI just ingests data and recognizes patterns in that data. When you query an AI model, it parses your words and tries to figure out what you're asking for and then searches its database of information to generate its response. The quality of the resulting output depends heavily on what data and instructions you provide in your prompt.

**NOTE**   To extract meaning from the words in a prompt, AI tools employ a technology called *natural language processing*, or NLP. NLP uses context mapping, pattern matching, and other techniques to determine the most likely meaning of a given user input.

And that's why prompt engineering is so important. The more you think about what you want in advance—the better you *engineer* your prompt—the better an AI model can follow your instructions and provide the output you want.

## AI Can't Read Your Mind

Here's another reason why prompt engineering is important: AI can't read your mind. AI is pretty good at following instructions, so if your instructions (that is, your prompts) are vague or incomplete, the AI is forced to guess at the details of what you want.

In this fashion, AI is a lot like us human beings. If we're forced to guess what someone wants, we stand a very good chance of guessing incorrectly. It's the same thing with AI: provide an overly vague prompt, and the AI will try to guess what you really meant or wanted. It won't always guess right.

Consider the following example. When you enter the prompt, **tell me about bats**, the AI model won't know whether you're talking about the flying mammal or the thing you hit a baseball with. It also won't know whether this information is for a grade school report, a social media post, or a scientific paper. And what, exactly, do you want to know about bats—how they work, their history, their role in society, or something else? You see the problem; with too little information, it's too easy to provide you with something that isn't at all what you want.

Here's another one. Let's say you want an AI image generator to create a picture of a cat. If you provide a simple prompt, such as **generate a picture of a cat**, the AI is forced to guess not only the type of cat but also the setting and the type of output. As you can see in Figure 2.1, the AI output is going to be all over the place with all sorts of cats doing all sorts of things. And each time you rerun that prompt, you'll get even more different results.

**FIGURE 2.1**

*Midjourney's response to the simple prompt for a picture of a cat.*

You get much better results when you provide a more detailed prompt. Note how the following revised prompt describes the type of cat, hair and eye color, setting, and output:

**Generate a photorealistic image of an orange long-haired cat with one green eye and one blue eye, sitting on a single bed with a blue bedspread in a bedroom with dusty light filtering in from a window on the right.**

As you can see in Figure 2.2, the results are much more precise than with the shorter prompt, even in the variations. You want even more control over the details, like what's in the background or how the cat is posing? Then add more details to the prompt.

**FIGURE 2.2**

*Midjourney's response to a more detailed prompt for a photorealistic image of an orange cat on a bed.*

This is a key factor in effective prompt engineering—figuring out what details to include in a prompt to generate the results you desire. The more details you provide, the more you're going to like the output.

Just remember, AI doesn't know what you want until you tell it. It can't read your mind, and any guesses it makes are likely to be way off base. The more precise your prompts, the more accurate the results.

## Bad Prompts = Bad Output

Constructing AI prompts is a little like constructing a search query for Google and other search engines. If you don't ask the right questions, you won't get the right answers.

It's all a matter of garbage in, garbage out. Provide an AI model with a prompt that is inexact, inaccurate, or just plain confusing, and AI will, more often than not, give you back something that is equally inexact, inaccurate, or confusing. If you don't know what you want, or don't know how best to word your request, AI will try to figure out what you're asking for—but probably won't get it right.

What constitutes a garbage prompt? There are a number of ways a prompt can be less than ideal:

- Too broad or vague (example: **make it pretty**)
- No clear goal or output format (example: **write something about classical music**)
- Missing necessary context (example: **analyze this** [without providing how you want the thing analyzed])
- Unrealistic instructions (example: **make this go viral**)
- Conflicting or confusing instructions (example: **make it sound casual and fun but also formal and professional**)
- Cramming too many tasks into a single prompt (example: **summarize this article, fix the grammar, turn it into a blog post, and generate an image**)

Bad prompts like these will almost guarantee that you won't be satisfied with the results. The better your prompts, the better the results.

## Good Prompts = Good Output

As you can see, prompt engineering is important because it determines how satisfied you'll be with what AI does. Creating better, more detailed prompts not only generates better results, but it also saves you time that you might otherwise spend redoing less-effective prompts. Effective prompt engineering also increases your productivity and creativity and ensures greater accuracy with fewer mistakes—and irrelevant hallucinations.

In short, good prompts create good output. That's what prompt engineering is all about.

# How to Turn a Bad Prompt into a Better Prompt

In most instances, the key to turning a bad prompt into a better prompt is simply to provide more detail. Use the prompt engineering strategies you'll learn in this book to provide very detailed instructions to the AI model, and you'll get significantly better results.

To that end, Table 2.1 provides some examples of bad prompts (vague, incomplete, and so on) turned into good prompts via prompt engineering.

**TABLE 2.1**   Examples of Bad Prompts Made Better

| Bad Prompt | Better Prompt |
| --- | --- |
| Write a cool Facebook post | Write a humorous Facebook post about working out at the gym this morning |
| Tell me about birds | Write 500 words about the major bird species |
| Write a report about black holes | Write a five-page scholarly report for my high school class about what black holes are, how they're formed, and how we detect them. Include citations in MLA format |
| Make it better | Edit the following passage to make it sound more confident and professional |
| Explain this to me like I'm dumb | Explain the following concept to me in terms a 6th grader can understand |
| Make a list of snacks | Create a list of affordable, low-carb snacks available at a typical grocery store |
| Recipe for dinner | Generate a recipe for an Italian main dish for four, featuring pasta and chicken |
| Tell me a joke | Tell me a joke about airplane travel in the style of Jerry Seinfeld |
| Picture of a girl | Create a photorealistic image of a grade-school girl with red hair and pigtails playing on a school playground |

You get the idea. Anything too vague is a bad prompt. Include more details and explicit instructions to make a prompt better and more effective.

# Summary

In this chapter, you learned what prompt engineering is and why it's important. You learned that an AI prompt is the way you communicate with AI tools and that the more detailed your prompt, the more satisfied you'll be with the output. Prompt engineering is all about creating accurate and detailed instructions for an AI model to follow; the better your instructions, the better the results.

IN THIS CHAPTER

- Crafting an effective AI prompt
- Necessary components of an AI prompt
- What *not* to include in a prompt
- Putting it all together

3

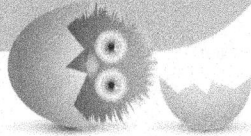

# THE ANATOMY OF A PERFECT PROMPT

AI prompt engineering is all about crafting more effective AI prompts, but how exactly do you do that? Not surprisingly, the most effective prompts contain similar key elements. Include these elements, and you'll likely be more satisfied with the AI results.

# Crafting an Effective AI Prompt

Crafting an effective AI prompt requires a clear understanding of what you want to receive and some forethought on how to best instruct the AI model to give you what you want. That's what prompt engineering is all about—engineering an effective prompt.

To be effective, your prompt needs to tell the AI model what you want it to do, how you want it to do it, and how you want it to present the results. You need to present these instructions in as much detail as necessary, while also being as concise as possible. (That's contradictory, I know; when in doubt, err on the side of too much detail.)

Doing this requires a little homework. Just entering a bunch of words off the top of your head isn't prompt engineering, it's freeforming—and it isn't consistently effective. You need to think about what you want the AI to do and then figure out the best way to instruct it to do that.

You might even want to write your prompt in advance, so that you can edit it as you work through it. Read through your prompt, one step or item at a time, and make sure it makes sense to you. If you get confused, so will the AI tool. Make the effort to ensure that your prompt is as clear as possible and includes all the necessary instructions and information.

Bottom line: Think of your prompt as a set of instructions that the AI will follow precisely. Make sure you're explaining things as clearly as possible and don't leave anything to chance.

# Necessary Components of an AI Prompt

Whether you're asking for text, image, or video output, your AI prompt needs to include the same basic components. These components include

- **Task:** What you want the AI to do, such as "write a..." or "summarize this..." or "generate a...," in as much detail as possible.
- **Format:** What kind of output you need, including length, type (blog post, letter, and so on), file format, and any other pertinent details.
- **Topic:** The thing in which you're interested. The subject of the verb presented in the task—write a paper about *topic*, answer a question about *topic*, or create a photo of a *topic*.
- **Tone or style:** Serious, lighthearted, professional, and so on.

- **Context:** Background information and relevant details about the topic, audience, or situation.

- **Requirements or constraints:** Things that the AI should include or exclude from the task.

We'll look at each of these elements in more detail next.

# Task

Probably the most important part of a prompt is the task or objective—what you want the AI to do. This is the primary directive to the AI tool, in as much detail and specificity as possible.

Start out by using action verbs, such as

- Write (a blog post, an email, a short story, and so on)

- Explain (a topic or concept)

- Tell me about (a topic)

- Generate (ideas, a list, an outline)

- Create (a photorealistic image, a watercolor painting, a short film)

- Summarize (a document, a piece of text, meeting notes)

- Analyze (a document, a piece of text, a web page, a report)

- Translate (a word, a phrase, a document)

- Compare (two documents, two pieces of text, two approaches or theories)

# Format

The format describes, in as much detail as possible, the type of output you want. It can be rather broad, such as an **article**, **story**, or **social media post**. But it should also include other necessary details, such as

- Length (number of words or pages or, for an audio or video, amount of time)

- File format

- Number of paragraphs or number of sections

- Number of slides (for a presentation)

- Aspect ratio or dimensions (for an image or video)

- Professional formats (such as MLA or APA format for scholarly papers)

The format might also specify how you want the output structured, such as in a bulleted or numbered list, Q&A format, and so forth. If the result should include specific sections, such as an introduction or summary, notate that as well.

> **NOTE**   Learn more about specifying different output formats in Chapter 4, "Defining Output in Your Prompts."

## Topic

Every task should reference a specific topic or target. The topic is typically a noun with one or more descriptive adjectives.

The topic follows the task and the format. As an example, the task might be **write**, the format might be **a blog post**, and the topic would be what you want the post to be about, such as **adopting a pet**. Put it all together, and you get the prompt:

**write a blog post about adopting a pet**

The more specific the topic, the better. For example, instead of saying

**write about banks**

say

**write about the history and different types of American banking institutions**

Instead of saying:

**create a picture of a girl**

Describe the subject in more detail as

**create a picture of a teenaged girl with long blonde hair and blue eyes wearing an orange t-shirt**

Along the same lines, instead of saying

**create a menu for dinner**

say

**Create a menu for dinner for four that includes appetizer, main course, and dessert and is gluten-free. Attendees prefer something light Mediterranean influenced.**

Instead of saying

**generate an outline for a detective story**

Provide more details, such as

**generate an outline for a detective story about a missing wife, mobsters, and an insurance scam, set in Chicago in the 1940s**

The more details you can include about your topic, the better.

## Tone and Style

With this element, you tell the AI what type of tone or style in which you want the results presented. This one isn't necessarily mandatory, but it can help steer the AI toward the desired results.

When describing the desired tone, you can use words such as *professional*, *friendly*, *witty*, *persuasive*, *formal*, *casual*, *academic*, *conversational*, or *concise*. When it comes to style, use descriptors such as *dark*, *dramatic*, *comedic*, *pompous*, and the like. You can even reference defined dramatic styles, such as **create a hardboiled mystery story** or **write a poem in the style of Robert Frost**. Use whatever descriptors you need to convey how you want your results presented.

## Context

Think of context as important background information that can help the AI model fine-tune its results. This background info might include details about the situation or characters, key facts about a given topic, important data points, where an image or video takes place, and the like.

## Requirements/Constraints

This element details things that must be included in the output or should not be included in the output. For example, if you're writing a paper for school, you can specify that the paper includes citations, a specific number of sources, and a summary or conclusion. You can specify elements or ideas that must be included, such as pointing to relevant data or arguments that should be referenced. For images, you also specify items that should be included in an image, such as background details and overall color scheme.

You can also specify things that should be avoided in the results, such as to avoid technical jargon, avoid inappropriate language or images, avoid mentioning specific arguments or approaches, or avoid mentioning particular individuals or groups. For images, you can also define colors or details to avoid.

In addition, you can note the intended audience for the output, as well as the desired reading level, such as **write an article at an 8th grade reading level** or **present the information in a way that 4th graders can understand it.**

## Optional Elements

There are also several optional elements you can include in a prompt as appropriate for the task at hand and the type of output you desire. These elements include

- **Goal:** If the objective is to persuade an audience to action or achieve some sort of response, let the AI know. For example, you might insert the goal of **convince the reader to vote for the proposal** or **lead the reader to request a sample** or something similar.

- **Role:** Ask the AI to assume a specific identity or perspective or describe the likely consumer of the output. For example, you might include something like **assume the role of a drill sergeant** or **assume you're teaching a high school class** or **write as if you're a seasoned political analyst**. Or, to detail the role of the consumer, you might include something like **direct the output to seniors considering Medicare plans** or **assume the readers are students at a liberal arts college**.

  **NOTE**  Learn more about having AI assume a specific role in Chapter 9, "Using Role-Based Prompting."

- **Examples and references:** One or more similar items that can serve as a reference for what type of output you want. You can use a specific URL to direct the AI to content on the web; cut and paste the example or reference into your prompt; or, with some AI tools, upload the reference as a separate file.

  **NOTE**  Learn more about using examples and references in Chapter 13, "Using Multimodal Prompts."

Which of these optional elements you include, if any, depends on the type of output you desire.

# What *Not* to Include in a Prompt

Knowing what not to include in an AI prompt is just as important as knowing what to include. To ensure better results, here are some things to avoid in your prompts:

- **Too many tasks at once:** AI models, just like us human beings, can get confused or overwhelmed if tasked to do too many things at the same time. If what you want is overly complex, break it down into multiple prompts.

- **Too many details or too much background information:** Similarly, you can overwhelm some AI models by including too many irrelevant background details. Include what's important or necessary, but don't make the model try to extract the wheat from the unnecessary chaff.

- **Contradictory instructions:** Don't ask the AI to go in two different directions at the same time. Your desired output cannot be both serious and light-hearted at the same time, nor can it be concise and detailed. Pick your lane and stick to it.

- **Jargon and industry speak:** Use plain English when crafting your prompt. Avoid lingo and TLAs (three-letter acronyms) that only industry insiders will understand. Don't assume the AI knows all the jargon used inside your company or industry.

- **Inappropriate or sensitive content:** Avoid asking for or referencing anything illegal, violent, or discriminatory. (You may, in fact, be prohibited from entering inappropriate prompts with some AI engines.)

- **Copyrighted material:** Along the same lines, avoid infringing on any copyrighted characters or material. While some AI engines might let you generate an image of Superman at your birthday party, others will refuse to do so on copyright grounds.

When it comes to crafting your prompts, just use common sense. Don't do anything confusing or inappropriate, and you should be fine.

# Putting It All Together

Now that you know what you should and shouldn't include in an AI prompt, let's put it all together to look at how to construct a complete prompt. Referencing all the previously discussed elements, follow this format:

**[task] [format] [topic] [tone] [context] [requirements/constraints] [optional elements]**

For example, if you want to write a college-level paper about the Revolutionary War, you can identify the elements shown in Table 3.1.

**TABLE 3.1**  Elements of a Prompt for a Scholarly Paper

| Element | Example |
|---------|---------|
| Task | Write a paper |
| Format | 1,000 words in MLA format |
| Topic | Revolutionary War |
| Tone | Scholarly |

| Element | Example |
|---|---|
| Context | Audience of college history professors |
| Requirements/constraints | Include information about the role of the Founding Fathers |
| Optional elements | Convince the audience to provide additional funding for my research |

Now all you have to do is put all that together in a prompt. Here's what that might look like:

**Write a 1,000-word paper in MLA format about the Revolutionary War. Use a scholarly tone appropriate for an audience of college history professors and include information about the role of the Founding Fathers. The goal is to convince the audience to provide additional funding for my research.**

Figure 3.1 shows the beginning of the paper, as written by ChatGPT.

> **The Revolutionary War and the Founding Fathers: A Critical Reassessment**
>
> The American Revolutionary War (1775–1783) stands not merely as a military confrontation between Great Britain and its North American colonies but as a crucible in which modern political thought, constitutional government, and national identity were forged. While popular historical narratives have long celebrated the war's drama and idealism, a deeper scholarly investigation reveals a more intricate tapestry of philosophical ambition, strategic diplomacy, and internal discord. At the center of this narrative lie the Founding Fathers—figures such as George Washington, Thomas Jefferson, John Adams, Benjamin Franklin, James Madison, and Alexander Hamilton—whose complex roles as revolutionaries, politicians, and thinkers demand a more nuanced analysis. This paper argues that sustained research into the Revolutionary War, with particular focus on the ideological and strategic contributions of the Founding Fathers, remains not only relevant but essential to understanding the genesis of American political culture. I seek additional funding to expand this line of inquiry, especially through archival work and historiographic reevaluation.
>
> The traditional historiography of the Revolutionary War has often leaned toward hagiography, elevating the Founding Fathers to quasi-mythical status. Yet, in recent decades, revisionist historians have begun to deconstruct these figures, examining the contradictions between their revolutionary ideals and their personal or political practices (Wood 12; Holton 47). For example, Thomas Jefferson's authorship of the Declaration of Independence in 1776—a document espousing equality and liberty—stands in stark contrast to his lifelong enslavement of African Americans. Likewise, George Washington's evolution from colonial officer to commander-in-chief of the Continental Army reflects both strategic brilliance and calculated image management (Chernow 103). A more thorough examination of these tensions can shed light on the ideological undercurrents of the Revolution and how ↓ . war's leaders reconciled, or failed to reconcile, principle with practice.

**FIGURE 3.1**

*The opening paragraphs of a scholarly paper about the Revolutionary War, as created by ChatGPT.*

Follow this format to create prompts for all types of tasks. As another example, let's say you want to create a short story for a six-year-old boy about superheroes in his neighborhood. Table 3.2 details the necessary elements.

**TABLE 3.2**   Elements of a Prompt for a Children's Story

| Element | Example |
|---|---|
| Task | Tell me a bedtime story |
| Format | Less than five minutes long |
| Topic | Superheroes in our neighborhood |
| Tone | Lighthearted |
| Context | For a six-year-old boy |
| Requirements/constraints | Not scary |
| Optional elements | Help put the boy to sleep |

And here's the resulting prompt:

**Tell me a bedtime story less than five minutes long about superheroes in our neighborhood for a six-year-old boy. The tone should be lighthearted, not scary, and help put the boy to sleep.**

Figure 3.2 shows the beginning of just such a story, as written by DeepSeek.

> The Sleepy Superheroes of Sunny Street
>
> One quiet evening on Sunny Street, as the moon rose high and the stars began to twinkle, six-year-old Max snuggled under his blanket. But just before he closed his eyes, he heard a tiny *whoosh* outside his window.
>
> Curious, Max peeked out and gasped—there, in the soft glow of the streetlight, was **Captain Pillow**, the sleepiest superhero of all! His fluffy cape billowed as he stretched and yawned.
>
> "Time for my bedtime patrol," Captain Pillow mumbled, floating gently down the street.
>
> Then, *zip!* **Pajama Girl** zoomed by in her striped slippers, delivering warm milk to anyone still awake. "Night-night, neighbors!" she whispered.
>
> Max giggled as **Blanket Boy** rolled past like a cozy burrito, tucking in stray puppies and sleepy cats. "Snuggle tight!" he murmured.
>
> Finally, **The Lullaby** floated down from the sky, strumming her guitar and singing a soft, soothing song. ⌄
> One by one, the houses on Sunny Street sighed and drifted off to sleep.

**FIGURE 3.2**

*The first part of a bedtime story about superheroes, as conceived by DeepSeek.*

You can also use this approach to create prompts for images, videos, and music. For example, if you want to generate a photo of an older couple at the dinner table for a marketing brochure, you'd use the elements shown in Table 3.3.

**TABLE 3.3**   Elements of a Prompt to Create a Photographic Image

| Element | Example |
| --- | --- |
| Task | Generate |
| Format | Photorealistic image in portrait format |
| Topic | Older couple sitting next to each other at a dinner table |
| Tone | Warm |
| Context | For a marketing brochure |
| Requirements/constraints | The couple should be holding hands and smiling. |
| Optional elements | Selling life insurance |

Here's the resulting prompt:

**Generate a photorealistic image in landscape format of an older couple sitting next to each other at a dinner table. The vibe should be warm and appropriate for a marketing brochure. The couple should be holding hands and smiling. The goal is to help sell life insurance.**

Figure 3.3 shows just one of the images generated by Midjourney from this prompt.

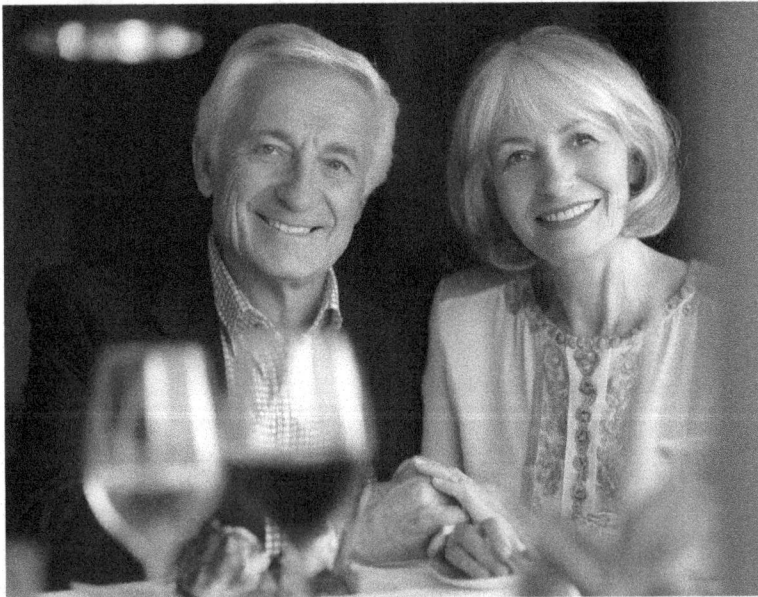

**FIGURE 3.3**

*A photorealistic image of an older couple at the dinner table, as generated by Midjourney.*

As you can see, when you follow this format and include the proper elements, you get pretty good results. It's a good place to start with your prompt engineering.

And, to help you get started, here's a blank form you can copy and use for your own prompt construction. It's labeled as Table 3.4, but it's really a prompt element template for your use.

**TABLE 3.4**   Prompt Element Template

| Element | Your prompt |
| --- | --- |
| Task | |
| Format | |
| Topic | |
| Tone | |
| Context | |
| Requirements/constraints | |
| Optional elements | |

# TIPS FOR MORE EFFECTIVE AI PROMPTS

Want to make your prompts even better? Then consider these quick tips for more effective prompts:

- Be as specific as possible.
- Use clear and concise language.
- Provide context or other background information that might be useful.
- Include any necessary requirements or constraints.
- Provide examples, in the form of similar files or the type of person who is writing or consuming the item.
- Ask for multiple options and then choose the best result given.
- Break complex tasks into multiple steps or multiple prompts.
- Use follow-up prompts to refine the results.
- Ask the AI tool to analyze and improve its own results.

As you can see, there are a lot of little things you can do to guarantee better AI results. For even more tips, check out Chapter 21, "Advanced Prompting Strategies and Tools."

# Summary

In this chapter, you learned the anatomy of an effective AI prompt. You learned how to craft a prompt and the essential elements to include. You also learned what *not* to include and how to put it all together in a practical fashion.

Next up, more information on how to use prompts to define your desired output.

4

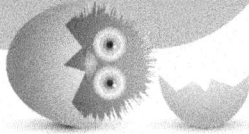

# DEFINING OUTPUT IN YOUR PROMPTS

For an AI model to know how to answer your question or fulfill your request, it needs to know how you want to receive its results. That is, the AI needs to know what type of output you want. If you want a multipage scholarly report, you don't want the AI to deliver a 200-word Facebook post.

To ensure that an AI model delivers the output the way you want it, you need to include output specifications in your prompts. You have to tell your AI how long the response should be, in what format and style, at what level of detail, and more. Without this information, the AI model won't know what kind of response to deliver.

# What Is Output Specification in an AI Prompt?

The process of telling AI what kind of output you want is called output specification. What exactly is output specification? At its most basic, output specification goes beyond what you say (the task element in a prompt) to how to say it. In essence, you're instructing the AI to give you a particular type of answer, in a particular way.

As with all things AI, consider output specification as if you're providing instructions to someone on how to deliver a task. Think of yourself as a teacher instructing your students how you want to receive their term papers—the length, the format, the style, and the like. Or think of yourself as a manager telling an employee how you want a job done—what constitutes successful completion. You don't leave the details to their imaginations; you tell them exactly what you expect.

It's the same way with AI. To guarantee the type of results you want or need, you have to include detailed output specifications in your prompts. AI is very good at following instructions, so make sure your instructions include the type and format of output you want.

# Why Is Output Specification Important?

Output specification is important because AI can't read your mind. If you don't ask for a specific type of output, it'll give you what it thinks you want—which may or may not be what you actually wanted.

Output specification in an AI prompt ensures that the results you get are usable and that they fit your needs. The wrong type of output may contain good information that can't easily be used for the task at hand.

As an example, let's say you're tasked with writing an article for your company or neighborhood newsletter. Consider a prompt with no output instructions, like this:

**write an article about local recycling resources**

The results may be usable, but they may not. The writing level may be too high or too low, the article may be too long or too short—you just don't know because the AI model didn't know. With no instructions, it has to guess, and it will probably guess wrong.

Instead, include detailed output specifications to create a prompt like this:

**write a 500-word article for a neighborhood newspaper about local recycling resources, at an 8th grade reading level**

That prompt will produce an article that matches what your editors expect.

Remember, vague or nonexistent output specifications often result in unhelpful or unacceptable results. You should never assume that AI knows what you mean. If you leave the AI wiggle room to interpret your instructions, you probably won't get the type of output you need. Always—*always*—specify the desired output in as much detail as possible.

# Types of Output to Specify

When it comes to specifying output, what parameters should you include? There are a number, and they depend on what type of output you want to create.

## Format

Let's start with the output format. Whether you're creating text, image, audio, or video content, there are lots of different formats you can use. You need to tell the AI model what format to create.

If you're creating text content, Table 4.1 details the types of output specifications you can include.

**TABLE 4.1**  Text Output Specifications

| Specification | Options |
| --- | --- |
| Social media post | Which social media network—Facebook, Twitter/X, LinkedIn, Instagram, TikTok, or others |
| Blog post | Type of blog—personal, business, and so on |
| Article | Type of media—newspaper, magazine, newsletter, website |
| Email | Personal or professional |
| Letter | Personal or professional |
| Report | School, business, scientific, and so on |
| Story | Fiction genre—science fiction, romance, mystery, or other |

If you're generating an image, consider the output specifications in Table 4.2.

**TABLE 4.2**  Image Output Specifications

| Specification | Options |
| --- | --- |
| Type of image | Photo, drawing, painting, and so on |
| Orientation | Portrait, landscape, square |
| Aspect ratio | 4:3, 16:9, or other |

If you're using AI to generate a video, consider the output specifications in Table 4.3.

**TABLE 4.3**  Video Output Specifications

| Specification | Options |
| --- | --- |
| Resolution | 720p, 1080p, 4K, and so on |
| Aspect ratio | 16:9, 4:3, or others |
| Orientation | Portrait, landscape, square (for TikTok) |
| Frame rate | 24 fps, 30 fps, 60 fps, and so on |
| File format | MP4, MOV, and others |

Finally, if you're using AI to create a song, use the output specifications in Table 4.4.

**TABLE 4.4**  Music Output Specifications

| Specification | Options |
| --- | --- |
| Tempo | In BPM |
| Key | Include major or minor |
| Audio format | Stereo or mono |
| File format | MP3, WAV, MIDI, and so on |

Bottom line, don't make the AI guess what you want—especially if what you want is slightly outside the norm. If left to their own devices, most AI models will default to fairly standard or popular formats, and that may not be what you want.

# Length/Size

It's important that you specify the length or size you want the AI model to create. How you do this depends on the type of output you're creating, as detailed in Table 4.5.

**TABLE 4.5**  Specifications for Length/Size

| Type of Output | Specifications |
| --- | --- |
| Text | Number of characters, sentences, paragraphs, pages, or sections |
| Images | Resolution of the image (in pixels per side) or size of the image (in inches per side) |
| Videos | Length |
| Presentations | Number of slides or total length of the presentation |
| Speeches | Amount of time you're allotted to speak |
| Music | Song length (sometimes it's desirable to provide a minimum and/or maximum length) |

So, for example, you might specify a

- 100-word Facebook post
- Five-page report
- 5" × 7" photograph
- Three-minute video
- 15-minute speech

## Tone and Style

Whatever type of output you're generating, it's important to relate the desired tone and style. That might mean:

- Professional versus casual
- Formal versus conversational
- Serious versus humorous
- Bright versus dark
- For AI-generated images, specify the art style (realistic, impressionistic, watercolor, cartoony)
- For AI-generated videos, specify the visual style (cinematic, film noir, animated)
- For AI-generated songs, specify the musical genre (rock, country, hip hop)

Use multiple descriptors, as necessary.

## Amount of Detail

Sometimes it's useful to tell AI how much detail should be included in the output. You can do this in general terms, such as

**provide a high-level overview**

or

**include detailed steps**

Or you can provide more explicit instructions, such as

**create a 3-level outline**

or

**include all relevant counterarguments**

## Point of View and Voice

You can also specify the point of view or voice in which to write the response. For example, you can specify writing in either the first, second, or third person. You can also tell the AI to write in either the active or passive voice.

For some types of output, it may help the AI to provide it with a persona from which to approach the writing. Just tell it to write or think like a particular person or type of person, such as

**write like a college professor**

or

**explain this like a professional chef**

> **NOTE**  You may need to combine multiple instructions (format, tone, length, etc.) to describe the desired output.

# Best Practices for Specifying Output

Let's put all this together and look at best practices for specifying output in AI prompts. In general, you should

- Know what elements you need to define for the type of output you want.
- Include information about format, length/size, tone and style, the amount of detail desired, and point of view and voice.
- Spell everything out in detail. Don't make the AI try to fill in the blanks.
- Be unambiguous. Don't leave room for interpretation.
- Use multiple descriptors, as necessary.

# Summary

In this chapter, you learned why it's important to specify output parameters in your AI prompts and which elements to specify. You learned the various ways to specify the output format, length and size, tone and detail, and other key elements. You also learned that you often need to combine multiple descriptors to obtain the appropriate type of output.

# UNDERSTANDING AND COMPARING DIFFERENT PROMPTING STRATEGIES

There are many different ways to approach crafting AI prompts. You can completely freeform it by putting together a prompt off the top of your head, or you can use one of several proven strategies designed specifically for different types of tasks.

Prompt engineering requires learning and then selecting the right prompting strategies for your specific needs. These prompting strategies help you generate more useful and accurate results from the AI models you use.

# Different Approaches to AI Prompting

There are six primary strategies you can use when engineering your AI prompts. The names may sound a little technical, but the strategies themselves are relatively easy to learn and use.

What are the major prompting strategies? In no certain order, they include

- Zero-shot
- One-shot
- Few-shot
- Role-based
- Chain-of-thought
- Self-consistency

We'll examine each of these strategies in the following sections and in their own chapters later in this book. Each strategy employs a different approach to constructing prompts—and uses different elements in different ways.

## Zero-Shot Prompting

Zero-shot prompting is the type of prompting with which you're probably most accustomed. With zero-shot prompting, all you do is describe the task at hand. You don't include any examples, just tell the AI model what you want it to do.

Zero-shot prompting can be freeform or structured, using the basic elements I described in Chapter 3, "The Anatomy of a Perfect Prompt." I prefer more structured prompts for most tasks, as using standard elements delivers more consistently superior results. But for quick and dirty tasks, such as asking simple questions, freeforming can also work.

What does a zero-shot prompt look like? Well, it looks like any of the prompts discussed in Chapter 3. You simply tell the AI model what you want it to do, with the appropriate level of detail.

Some examples of zero-shot prompts include

**write a short story about a robot who falls in love**

**create a recipe for a vegan version of pad thai**

Note that none of these examples reference any examples, either descriptively or in an accompanying file or web page.

The strengths of zero-shot prompting are that it is fast, simple, and efficient. You don't have to learn any fancy techniques other than the basic elements of a prompt.

The downside of zero-shot prompting is that it leaves too much interpretation in the hands of the AI model. Without examples of what you want, the AI may misinterpret your intent or miss important context. It's guessing at what you want.

Those pros and cons mean that zero-shot prompting is best for quick and easy tasks, for more creative tasks (where the AI has more latitude), and for those tasks where you provide well-defined output specifications. When there's no example to reference, you have to tell the AI exactly the type of output you want—or trust it to go off on its own.

> **NOTE**  Learn more about the zero-shot strategy in Chapter 6, "Using Zero-Shot Prompting."

## One-Shot Prompting

Our next prompting strategy is called one-shot prompting. In contrast to the zero-shot strategy, which utilizes no examples, one-shot prompting references an example in the prompt. That example can be included within the prompt (**write a poem in the style of Edgar Allen Poe's The Raven**) or in an accompanying file or webpage (**write an article about J.S. Bach in the style of the one at this webpage: [*URL*]**).

One-shot prompting is useful when the AI model needs more context than you can provide in just a few words. That's especially important with new or unusual tasks, or those tasks that require very specific output formatting.

The advantage of one-shot prompting is that it provides a very clear reference to the type of output you want, especially when instructions can be interpreted a number of ways. It's good for more complex or nuanced tasks, or for those tasks that require a set format. It's particularly important if you're working in a specific field, such as the medical or legal fields, where there are set conventions to follow and jargon to include.

The disadvantage of one-shot prompting is that it's a little more complicated than zero-shot prompting. You also have the task of finding an appropriate example to reference, which may not always be easy.

> **NOTE**  Learn more about the one-shot strategy in Chapter 7, "Using One-Shot Prompting."

## Few-Shot Prompting

If providing one example in your prompt isn't enough, you can provide one or more examples via the few-shot prompting strategy. Few-shot prompting gets the AI model going with a few solid examples and then lets it finish the job on its own.

Few-shot programming is good for tasks that require pattern recognition. As it builds on previous examples. For example, you could use few-shot programming to create an FAQ or a list of questions. Start out by providing the first two items and let the AI fill in the rest, like this:

**create a list of the capitals of countries in europe**

**Q: What is the capital of France?**

**A: Paris**

**Q: What is the capital of Germany?**

**A: Berlin**

**Q: What's the capital of Italy?**

**A:**

Figure 5.1 shows how ChatGPT finishes this task.

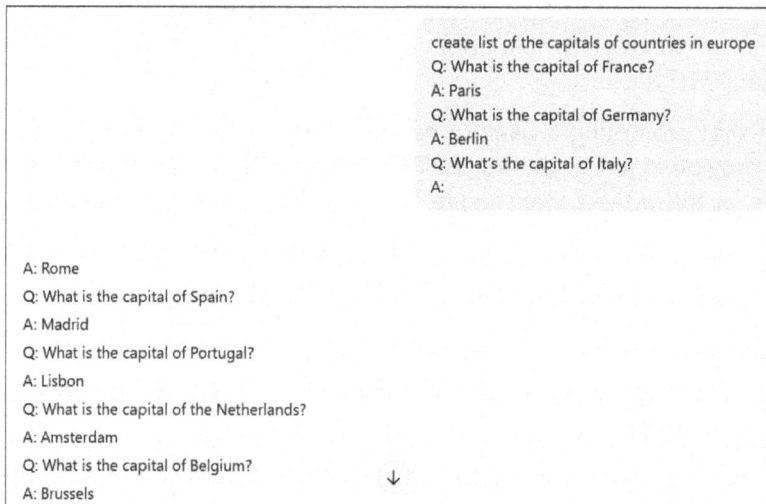

create list of the capitals of countries in europe
Q: What is the capital of France?
A: Paris
Q: What is the capital of Germany?
A: Berlin
Q: What's the capital of Italy?
A:

A: Rome
Q: What is the capital of Spain?
A: Madrid
Q: What is the capital of Portugal?
A: Lisbon
Q: What is the capital of the Netherlands?
A: Amsterdam
Q: What is the capital of Belgium?
A: Brussels

**FIGURE 5.1**

*ChatGPT completion of a few-shot prompt.*

The primary advantage of few-shot programming is that it helps train the AI on exactly how to proceed. The disadvantages are that you have to come up with a few examples on your own and that you end up creating longer and more complicated prompts.

**NOTE**  Learn more about the few-shot strategy in Chapter 8, "Using Few-Shot Prompting."

## Role-Based Prompting

Sometimes you get better results if you tell the AI model to assume a role or persona when providing an answer. This is called role-based prompting, and it helps to assign to the AI the tone or style (or even expertise) of a given individual or role.

For example, when creating output for school-age children, you might want to assign the AI the role of a teacher, like this:

**assume the role of an elementary school teacher and explain how clouds make it rain**

You can have AI assume any number of roles, from lawyers and doctors to customer service agents and mechanics. It's useful when crafting instructional tasks, simulating customer interactions, and in creative writing (**assume the role of a well-known mystery author**).

The primary strengths of role-based prompting are that it helps tailor responses to specific audiences and generate output that sounds like it was created by a specific person or type of person. That said, its primary weakness is that it can sometimes reproduce the biases or inaccurate knowledge of the persona assumed.

**NOTE**  Learn more about the role-based strategy in Chapter 9, "Using Role-Based Prompting."

## Chain-of-Thought Prompting

The next AI prompting strategy is called chain-of-thought prompting. With chain-of-thought prompting, you instruct the AI model to show its steps as it reasons through solving a problem. The AI then breaks down complex reasoning into manageable parts that you can more easily examine and learn from.

Chain-of-thought prompting is often used when solving math and logic problems, or in any instance that requires multistep reasoning.

The following prompt is an example of chain-of-thought prompting:

**Alice is older than Bob. Bob is older than Charlie. Who is the oldest? Think it through step by step.**

Figure 5.2 shows how Google Gemini answers this prompt in a step-by-step fashion.

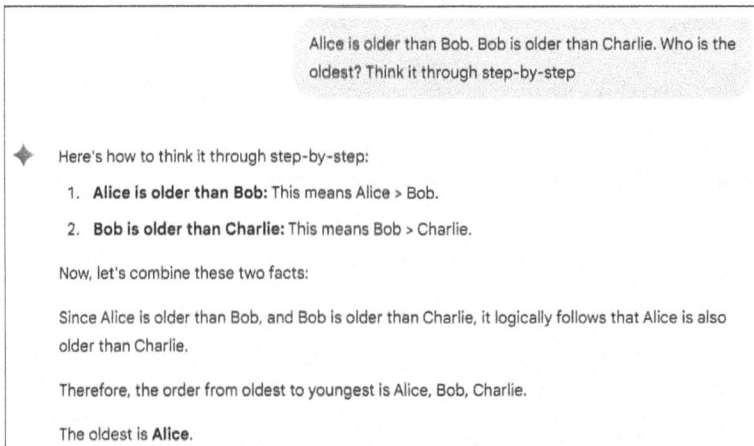

Alice is older than Bob. Bob is older than Charlie. Who is the oldest? Think it through step-by-step

Here's how to think it through step-by-step:

1. **Alice is older than Bob:** This means Alice > Bob.
2. **Bob is older than Charlie:** This means Bob > Charlie.

Now, let's combine these two facts:

Since Alice is older than Bob, and Bob is older than Charlie, it logically follows that Alice is also older than Charlie.

Therefore, the order from oldest to youngest is Alice, Bob, Charlie.

The oldest is **Alice.**

**FIGURE 5.2**

*Google Gemini's step-by-step response to a chain-of-thought prompt.*

The main strength of chain-of-thought prompting is that it improves the accuracy of complex tasks. The primary weakness is that chain-of-thought prompting can be verbose—and, sometimes, the AI model can "hallucinate" faulty reasoning.

**NOTE**   Learn more about the chain-of-thought strategy in Chapter 10, "Using Chain-of-Thought Prompting."

## Self-Consistency Prompting

The final prompting strategy is called self-consistency prompting. This strategy works by instructing the AI model to generate multiple reasoning paths and then select the most consistent answer.

You typically employ self-consistency prompting alongside chain-of-thought prompting. You use chain-of-thought prompts to generate the initial responses, then self-consistency prompting to determine the most common or logical outcome.

A typical self-consistency prompt might look something like this:

**Solve the following math problem using step-by-step reasoning. Then, repeat the process two more times using different paths to reach your answer. Afterward, identify the most common final answer. The problem is as follows:**

**A farmer has chickens and cows. In total, there are 30 heads and 100 legs. How many chickens and how many cows are there?**

As you can see, this creates a somewhat longer prompt than what you may be used to. The answer is also longer because the AI model should detail each of the paths generated, then select the most consistent answer.

Self-consistency prompting is best used for situations where complex reasoning is required.

The strengths of self-consistency prompting are that it improves accuracy and confidence in results. It's also a good way to reduce any hallucinations that might crop up with regular chain-of-thought prompting.

The strategy's weaknesses are that it requires longer prompts, is slower than other types of prompts, and is more resource intensive. Essentially, it's like running a single prompt multiple times.

> **NOTE**   Learn more about the self-consistency strategy in Chapter 11, "Using Self-Consistency Prompting."

# Comparing Prompting Strategies

Now that you know a little about all six major AI prompting strategies, let's look at them all together and evaluate their pros and cons. To that end, turn to Table 5.1, which compares the primary uses, pros, and cons of the prompting strategies.

**TABLE 5.1**   Comparison of Prompting Strategies

| Strategy | Best For | Pros | Cons |
| --- | --- | --- | --- |
| Zero-shot | Simple tasks | Fast, easy | Can leave much open for interpretation; inconsistent results |
| One-shot | Unusual formats | Adds important context | Requires researching and finding appropriate examples |
| Few-shot | Pattern recognition tasks, lists | Builds on examples | Creates lengthy prompts; requires you to come up with several examples first |

| Strategy | Best For | Pros | Cons |
|---|---|---|---|
| Chain-of-thought | Math, logic, and reasoning tasks | Spells out internal thinking and logic | May hallucinate steps |
| Role-based | Instructional tasks, simulating interactions, creative writing | Provides natural responses like a given person or role | Can exhibit biases of the persona assumed |
| Self-consistency | Complex reasoning | Improved reliability and confidence | Slower to run; requires more computing resources |

# Choosing the Right Prompting Strategy

Here's the thing with choosing a prompting strategy—there's no one-size-fits-all solution. No single strategy is ideal for all situations. Which prompting strategy you choose depends on the task, the intended audience, and the desired outcome.

That said, as a general rule of thumb, you can use zero-shot prompting for most basic tasks. Anything more complicated may require a more complicated prompting strategy.

Here are my recommendations:

- Use **zero-shot prompting** for simple requests, basic writing for personal use, answering questions, and chatting in real time with AI chatbots.

- Use **one-shot prompting** when specific output—especially scholarly, legal, or scientific output—is required.

- Use **few-shot prompting** when assembling lists and FAQs or when output must follow a specific format or reasoning pattern.

- Use **role-based prompting** when it's important to present answers as if from a specific individual or type of individual or when writing genre fiction.

- Use **chain-of-thought prompting** when understanding internal reasoning is important.

- Use **self-consistency prompting** for more critical or complicated reasoning tasks.

Obviously, that doesn't cover all contingencies, but it does get you in the ballpark.

In addition, know that you can combine different strategies to enhance your results. For example, you can combine role-based and chain-of-thought strategies to have the AI reason like a particular type of individual, like this:

**assume the role of a college philosophy professor and provide a step-by-step analysis of how the trolley problem works**

Bottom line: Employ whichever AI prompting strategy results in the best and most reliable results. That may require experimenting with different strategies until you find the best one. They're all good at different things.

# Summary

In this chapter, you learned about the six most common AI prompting strategies— zero-shot, one-shot, few-shot, role-based, chain-of-thought, and self-consistency prompting. You learned how each strategy works, what it's best for, and its pros and cons. Finally, you learned which strategy is best for specific types of tasks— and that you can sometimes combine multiple strategies to provide even better results.

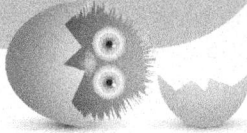

6

# USING ZERO-SHOT PROMPTING

Of the six major AI prompting strategies, zero-shot prompting is the easiest and most common. Zero-shot prompting is creating a prompt without providing any examples. It works when you trust that the AI model already knows how to do what you want it to do.

# What Zero-Shot Prompting Is and How It Works

In the world of AI, a "shot" is an example referenced in a prompt. Thus, one-shot prompting involves the use of a single example, few-shot prompting involves the use of a few examples, and zero-shot prompting—the topic of this chapter— involves zero examples.

That's right, a zero-shot prompt is a prompt that doesn't include or reference any examples. It's the kind of prompt that most people do all the time, a prompt that simply describes the task at hand, without having to reference other similar tasks or content.

You use zero-shot prompting when you can safely assume that the AI model knows what you're talking about. Alternatively, you can use it when you describe in the prompt what you want in detail.

Zero-shot prompting works (when it does—which is surprisingly often) because the AI model has been pretrained on data similar to the task at hand—which is a reasonable assumption, based on the tremendous size of most large language model datasets. The AI can then pull from that dataset the information it needs to complete the task at hand. If it doesn't find comparable data, or if it simply guesses wrong, then you need to rerun the prompt and provide more detail for the AI to go on.

# When to Use Zero-Shot Prompting

As I said, zero-shot prompting is all that most people know and do with today's AI models. That means that you already know how to create a zero-shot prompt—it's simply a prompt where you appropriately describe the task at hand and the output you desire, without providing any relevant examples of either.

The relative simplicity of zero-shot prompting makes it ideal for a wide variety of AI-related tasks, including

- Answering questions and providing quick facts
- Everyday productivity (summarizing text and meetings, generating ideas, and so on)
- Basic writing (letters, emails, social media posts)
- Comparisons and simple analysis
- Education and training
- Language translation
- Programming and application development (creating code)

What is zero-shot prompting *not* good for? Here's a short list of tasks that typically require more sophisticated prompting strategies:

- Complex tasks that require step-by-step reasoning
- Creating content where specific output formatting is required
- Tasks where accuracy or nuance is critical
- Writing genre fiction and similar content

# Crafting Effective Zero-Shot Prompts

How do you go about crafting a zero-shot prompt? It's all about using the techniques presented previously in this book.

> **NOTE**   Learn more about these other elements of a prompt in Chapter 3, "The Anatomy of a Perfect Prompt."

To refresh your memory, effective zero-shot prompting requires you to provide very detailed instructions, both about the task you want performed and how you want the output to look. Your prompts should include all or most of the following elements:

- Task, or what you want the AI to do
- Output format
- Topic
- Tone or style
- Context or background info
- Requirements or constraints

> **NOTE**   While prompts can include other elements, such as roles and examples, these are not typically included with zero-shot prompts. These elements are used in other prompting strategies.

In practice, that creates a prompt that looks something like the following (just replace the element in brackets with details of the task at hand):

**[task] [format] [topic] [tone] [context] [requirements/constraints] [optional elements]**

With that in mind, Table 6.1 details some common AI-related tasks and typical zero-shot prompts for each.

**TABLE 6.1** Examples of Zero-Shot Prompts

| Task | Example prompt |
| --- | --- |
| Business writing | Write a professional email turning down the employee's request for paid time off |
| Casual writing | Write an email to my Aunt Martha asking for her recipe for strawberry jam |
| Code generation | Write HTML code to insert and center an image |
| Comparisons | Compare the factors behind the American Revolution and the French Revolution |
| Creative writing | Write a short story about a time traveler visiting from the future |
| DIY tasks | How do I unclog the drain in my shower? |
| Editing/rewriting | Rewrite the following sentence to sound more formal: I'm hitting the clubs tonight with my homies. |
| Explain a concept | Explain how gravity works to an eight-year-old |
| Fact checking | Is it true that turkey's roost in trees? |
| Giving advice | How can I put screen limits on my teenager? |
| Idea generation | Generate five names for a new casual seafood restaurant |
| Poetry writing | Write a short poem about hummingbirds in the spring |
| Question answering | What is the capital of Montana? |
| Recipe generation | Give me a quick and easy recipe for meat-free lasagna |
| Report writing | Write a 5-page scholarly report at the college level about near-light travel, include at least six citations in MLA format |
| Simple math problems | What is the square root of 625? |
| Simplify language | Rewrite the following legal clause in plain English: The undersigned hereby acknowledges and agrees to the foregoing terms and conditions. |
| Social media posting | Create a Facebook post commenting on the summer weather in South Florida |
| Speech writing | Write a 5-minute speech to an audience of small business owners about the benefits of social media marketing |
| Summarizing | Summarize the plot of Ernest Hemingway's *The Sun Also Rises* |
| Teaching | Generate a lesson plan to teach 5th graders about recycling |
| Translating | Translate the following sentence into Spanish: Where is the nearest restaurant? |
| Travel planning | Create an itinerary for a three-day trip to Chicago for a first-time visitor |
| Workout plans | Create a workout routine for an ex-runner with knee problems |

There are obviously many more examples where those came from, but that should give you a good idea of how zero-shot prompting works. What all these examples have in common is their lack of examples—all the necessary information is included in the prompt itself, no other references necessary.

# Tips for Better Zero-Shot Prompting

Zero-shot prompting works for many, many tasks, but there are ways to improve your results. Consider these tips for producing better zero-shot prompting output:

- Address possible ambiguities in advance to avoid misinterpretation.
- Start with a simple prompt, analyze the results, and then add more detail in further iterations.
- Combine zero-shot and role-based prompting to generate results targeted at a specific audience.
- Combine zero-shot and chain-of-thought prompting to break down more complex tasks into smaller individual steps.
- Combine zero-shot and self-consistency prompting to generate multiple results and choose the best of those.

All of these tips will help you get better results from zero-shot prompting. Employ them as appropriate.

# Limitations of Zero-Shot Prompting

Zero-shot prompting isn't the best approach for all situations. This strategy has its drawbacks and limitations.

First, know that vague or ambiguous prompts can lead to unpredictable and often unacceptable results. The more you leave up to interpretation, the more likely it is that the AI model will guess wrong.

Similarly, the model's performance is highly sensitive to how the zero-shot prompt is posed. Slight changes in wording can significantly alter the AI's interpretation of the task.

In addition, the results of zero-shot prompting may not be as accurate as those from AI models trained for specific tasks. Put simply, zero-shot prompting isn't the best strategy for use with highly specialized or complex tasks that require more nuanced and defined understanding.

Here's another thing. Because you don't reference explicit examples, zero-shot prompting provides no opportunity for guided learning. You have to describe everything—and even the most detailed descriptions may not be enough.

Finally, as with all things AI, the potential exists for hallucinations when completing factual tasks. Don't blindly accept any AI results without double-checking their accuracy.

## COMPARING ZERO-SHOT TO OTHER PROMPTING STRATEGIES

How does zero-shot prompting compare to other AI prompting strategies? Zero-shot prompting is, at least on the surface, a simpler strategy than the other approaches, although that simplicity can often require a surfeit of details in the prompt description. I suppose one could say that it's simpler to envision and approach, even if it sometimes results in more complex prompts.

Compared to one-shot and few-shot prompting, zero-shot doesn't require you to come up with any examples. However, the results of zero-shot prompting can be less predictable than with those other strategies. That makes one-shot prompting better when you need extremely specific output, and few-shot better when you have a particular approach or format you want to replicate.

Compared to chain-of-thought and self-consistency prompting, zero-shot is simpler but also less suited for more complex, logic-based tasks. Use those other strategies when you have a multistep task and want to see the results of each step.

Finally, when comparing zero-shot prompting with role-based prompting, know that the role-based approach can lead to much more specific results—unless you describe your zero-based prompt in extreme detail. It's often easier to just have the AI assume a role and determine the proper content and output from there.

Bottom line, use the zero-shot strategy for simple tasks and those that you can clearly describe in the prompt. For anything more complex or requiring more specific output, switch to another more appropriate technique.

## Summary

In this chapter, you learned all about the most common prompting strategy, zero-shot prompting. You learned what zero-shot prompting is, how it works, and when best to use it. You also learned how to create effective zero-shot prompts and how zero-shot compares to other prompting strategies.

Next up: one-shot prompting!

7

# USING ONE-SHOT PROMPTING

In the previous chapter, you learned about zero-shot prompting—AI prompts that work purely via description, with no examples or references. Now it's time to see what happens when you provide an AI model with an example of what you want it to do. This is called one-shot prompting, and it's an effective strategy for many types of tasks.

# What One-Shot Prompting Is and How It Works

In the parlance of artificial intelligence, a "shot" is an example or reference. So zero-shot prompting uses no examples, and one-shot prompting uses a single example. (And, yes, there's a strategy that utilizes multiple examples; it's called few-shot prompting, and we'll discuss it in the next chapter.)

The key to one-shot prompting is to enhance a traditional zero-shot prompt by referencing an example of the output (either content or format) you desire. By providing a clear example of what you expect, this approach helps guide the AI's output and improve its performance.

One-shot prompting works like this:

1. Include an example of the task you want completed within your normal prompt.

2. The AI model uses this example to understand the context, task, or formatting.

3. The AI model generates a response following the example provided.

It all starts with your prompt. Craft a detailed prompt, as you would normally, but then reference an example within the prompt. That example can be entered into the prompt itself, included as a reference to a webpage URL, or attached as a file you upload to the AI model.

You can use said example to clarify the tone of the desired output, detail the output format, or delineate the specific requirements of the task. This reduces any potential ambiguity, improves the model's accuracy, and ensures the model follows specific style or formatting guidelines.

As to how one-shot prompting works, it's a matter of the AI learning by example—the example you provide. When you provide the AI model with an example, it uses that example to guide its results. The AI not only parses the instructions in your prompt but also analyzes the example to determine what to include in the results and how to present those results.

**NOTE**    Providing an example in a one-shot prompt is often easier than trying to describe what you want in words. (One example, like a picture, is sometimes worth a thousand words.) This makes one-shot prompting a more efficient approach for some tasks.

# When to Use One-Shot Prompting

When should you employ the one-shot prompting strategy? It's useful for the following types of tasks:

- Text generation
- Question answering
- Translation
- Summarization

When you're considering the use of one-shot prompting, you'll need a task where clear examples exist. If you're not sure what output you want, you won't be able to find an example to use. It also helps if the task has clear requirements for the type of output needed. If the output format is ill-defined or open ended, it would be difficult to choose an example to follow.

When should you employ the one-shot prompting strategy? It's often useful for text generation, question answering, translation, and summarization. It's also useful if you're having trouble defining the task or output. Providing an example can remove any confusion or ambiguity you might have over the task.

Know also that one-shot prompting is commonly used in more complex tasks and seldom with simpler requests. It's just not worth the effort if you need a response of only a sentence or two.

Finally, use one-shot prompting when zero-shot prompting doesn't provide acceptable results. Providing an example is just another way of adding more detail to your instructions, which is a good way to improve your results.

**NOTE**   One-shot prompting may not be ideal for creative tasks unless you're trying to emulate a specific work or style. With these types of tasks, it's better to let the AI have its head.

# How to Reference Examples in Prompts

There are several different ways to structure a one-shot prompt. Let's look at a few.

## Including Examples Within the Prompt

Perhaps the simplest type of one-shot prompt is one that includes an example within the prompt itself. With this approach, you provide an example of what you want alongside your task instructions, and then the AI model follows your example.

For example, if you want the AI model to translate a foreign-language phrase, you might provide the following prompt and example:

**Translate English to Spanish.**

**Example:**

**English: "Where is the library?"**

**Spanish: "¿Dónde está la biblioteca?"**

**Now translate:**

**"I would like a coffee."**

That's a little wordy, but it gets the job done.

Similarly, you could fashion a prompt that instructs the model to extract key information from a passage, like the following:

**Extract the name and occupation from the sentence.**
**Example:**
**"Dr. Angela Martin is a veterinarian in Denver."**
**Name: Angela Martin**
**Occupation: Veterinarian**

**Now extract:**
**"Marcus Reed is a 30-year-old firefighter from Austin who has a wife and three children."**

You can also use this approach in creative writing. Say, for example, you want an AI model to create a new joke like one you like. You might use the following prompt:

**Create a new joke like this one:**
**Why did the chicken cross the road? To get to the other side.**

## Referencing Examples Online

You can also reference specific websites or web pages as examples in a one-shot prompt. For this approach, simply include the URL of the example within the prompt, such as the following:

**Write a blog post about the song "Respect" in the style of posts at [URL]**

or

**Generate a report detailing the issues involved with recycling in the style of the report located at [URL]**

**NOTE**   Referencing online content doesn't always work because AI models might not have access to recent web pages.

## Referencing Well-Known Examples

Sometimes your example is sufficiently well-known that you can simply reference it by name. In this instance, all you have to do is reference the existing work, like in the following example:

**Write a short speech about the value of good citizenship in the style of John F. Kennedy's "New Frontier" speech**

or

**Put together a code of ethics using the same format as the Bill of Rights**

## Referencing Examples in an Accompanying File

Many AI models let you upload files (typically in .txt, .docx, or .pdf formats) that you can then use as examples for a prompt. This approach requires you to use the AI's upload tool to first upload the file and then reference it in your prompt.

Here's an example, after uploading an earlier blog post:

**Write a blog post in a similar style about helicopter parenting**

Or say you've uploaded an academic report that you want to use as a guide for your new task. Use a prompt like the following:

**Use the file as a formatting example and write a 1,000-word academic report about avian flu.**

# Best Practices for Creating Effective One-Shot Prompts

When it comes to crafting an effective one-shot prompt, reference these best practices:

- Select or create a representative example that is relevant to the task.
- Make sure the example is formatted according to the desired output.
- Make sure the example is clear and understandable, with no ambiguity.
- Make sure the example itself doesn't contain any errors.
- If creating an example, be as concise as possible.
- Ensure that the input you provide matches the format of the example.

- Clearly separate the example from the actual task prompt by using section headers or delimiters (commas, asterisks, and so on).

- Include only a single example.

> **NOTE**   Avoid misleading examples or those that exhibit any form of bias, or the results you get might also be biased.

# Advanced One-Shot Prompting Strategies

You can make one-shot prompting more effective by employing some advanced strategies. Consider the following:

- Run the same prompt but with different examples and choose the result that works best.

- Use iterative prompting by rewording and reworking the original prompt based on the original results.

- Add constraints (such as word count limits) to the example to fine-tune the task.

- For complex tasks, use prompt chaining along with one-shot examples.

- Combine one-shot prompting with role-based prompting for more individualized results.

- Combine one-shot prompting with chain-of-thought prompting to view the steps the AI takes to generate its results.

> **NOTE**   Learn about iterative prompts in Chapter 15, "Refining Your Prompts." Learn about prompt chaining in Chapter 12, "Using Prompt Chaining." Learn about role-based prompting in Chapter 9, "Using Role-Based Prompting." Learn about chain-of-thought prompting in Chapter 10, "Using Chain-of-Thought Prompting."

# Limitations of One-Shot Prompting

One-shot prompting isn't for everybody or every task. It definitely has its limitations.

One significant limitation of one-shot prompting concerns the AI model's sensitivity to the quality of the provided example. Since the AI model tries to fit its result to the example you provide, a poorly chosen example can lead to inaccurate or irrelevant outputs.

How well your prompt matches the example can also be problematic. AI models can struggle when the actual input in the prompt deviates from the example in terms of style, length, or structure. In this situation, the AI model might "overfit" the characteristics of the example. For example, if your example uses bullet points for a list, but your actual input uses numbered lists, the model might fail to properly extract the data.

In addition, one-shot prompting may struggle with highly complex tasks that require in-depth understanding or require multiple-step processes. In these instances, few-shot or chain-of-thought prompting may be more appropriate. This is also the case if the single example isn't detailed enough for the AI model to understand the underlying intent.

Finally, using preexisting examples in one-shot prompting can introduce the potential for bias in the AI results. If the example provided contains any inherent biases (such as racial or gender biases), the AI model is likely to pick up and amplify those biases in its output. It simply has no better examples to balance out the single example's bias.

## COMPARING ONE-SHOT TO OTHER SHOT-BASED PROMPTING STRATEGIES

How does one-shot prompting compare to other prompting strategies—especially the other shot-based approaches?

Compared to zero-shot prompting, the one-shot approach can provide a more exact output. Use one-shot prompting when you can't adequately explain the output you want in zero-shot text.

Compared to few-shot prompting, one-shot prompting is simpler to implement but may not produce as accurate a result, especially with complex tasks. When the task can't be guided through a single example, use few-shot prompting instead.

At the end of the day, the shot-based prompting method you choose requires you to make a trade-off in terms of accuracy and ease of effort. Zero-shot may be the easiest strategy to use, but one-shot and few-shot will often produce more precise results.

# Summary

In this chapter, you learned that one-shot prompting lets you guide an AI model by providing an example of what you want and how you want it. You learned how one-shot prompting works and the various ways to reference examples in your prompts. You also learned best practices and advanced strategies for one-shot prompting, as well as some of the limitations of this approach.

So, what's next after zero-shot and one-shot prompting? How about few-shot prompting, where you get to reference multiple examples in a prompt—which you'll learn about in the next chapter.

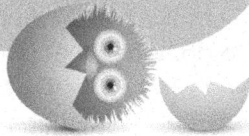

8

# USING FEW-SHOT PROMPTING

The previous two chapters covered zero-shot and one-shot prompting, how they work, and when to use them. That done, there's one more shot-based prompting strategy: few-shot prompting. It involves including multiple examples in a prompt, and you use it when a single example isn't enough.

# What Few-Shot Prompting Is and How It Works

Zero-shot prompting is a prompt with no examples. One-shot prompting is a prompt with one example. Few-shot prompting, then, is a prompt that includes a few examples.

Why might you need to include multiple examples in a prompt? It all depends on how much about the task at hand the AI model knows and whether you need very specific output. If the AI model is unlikely to know exactly what you want, including multiple examples helps guide it to the desired result.

It's the same rationale for using one-shot over zero-shot prompting. Zero-shot is good when the AI model has likely trained on similar content and can reliably interpret what you want it to do. When that isn't the case, you can guide the AI by providing it with an example to follow, which is what one-shot prompting does. When a single example might not be enough for the AI to learn from, use few-shot prompting and additional examples.

Few-shot prompting, then, helps AI understand the format, style, and content you want, without you needing to accurately describe all of that in a basic zero-shot prompt. The multiple examples should provide all the details the AI model needs.

A few-shot prompt typically includes a clear question or instruction, accompanied by two or more examples that show how the task should be completed. It works because AI models are trained to recognize patterns in text content and then continue those patterns. That helps train the model on the type of output you want.

> **NOTE**  How much is a few? When it comes to few-shot prompting, a few is defined as more than one. You can use as many examples as you need to get your point across, but you probably want to hold it to under a half dozen.

# When to Use Few-Shot Prompting

Because few-shot prompting requires more effort on your part than zero- or one-shot prompting, you probably won't be using it quite as often. When does few-shot prompting make sense? You should use it when

- Zero-shot or one-shot prompting doesn't generate acceptable results.
- The task contains nuanced elements, especially the way results should be presented.
- You need the output to contain a specific structure, formatting, style, or tone, as with official reports and documents.

- You need the output to consistently mirror the tone or style of existing material, as with marketing materials for an existing client.

- When exact working or phrasing is important, as in legal and medical papers.

- When the task involves specialized terminology or concepts not likely represented in the AI model's training data.

When might you *not* want to use few-shot prompting? You probably want to avoid using few-shot prompting for very simple and straightforward tasks, such as basic translation and answering simple questions. If you don't need to provide an example, then don't.

# How to Craft a Few-Shot Prompt

Crafting a few-shot prompt is similar to crafting a one-shot prompt. You need to include

- The task to be completed, in clear, concise language

- Two or more examples of the desired output, typically in the form of input/output pairs

- The new input for which you want the AI to generate a response

You can use this template:

**Task: [INSTRUCTION/TASK]**

**Example 1**
**Input: [EXAMPLE 1]**
**Output: [EXAMPLE 1]**

**Example 2**
**Input: [EXAMPLE 2]**
**Output: [EXAMPLE 2]**

**New input**
**[INPUT]**

Note that the inputs and outputs don't have to be labeled as such. For example, if you're asking an AI model to summarize an article, you might use the labels **Article** and **Summary** instead, as in the following example:

**Task: Condense a news article into a concise one-sentence summary, highlighting the main event and key players.**

Example 1

Article: "A pair of rare Amur tiger cubs made their public debut this week at the Minnesota Zoo, marking a significant victory for conservation efforts. The cubs, named Andrei and Amaliya, were born to parents Dari and Luka on May 23. Amur tigers were on the verge of extinction in the 1930s and 1940s but have recovered somewhat since then. The Minnesota Zoo has a long history of conserving tigers."

Summary: Two rare Amur tiger cubs, Andrei and Amaliya, were recently born at the Minnesota Zoo, representing a vital step forward in the conservation of this endangered species.

Example 2

Article: "San Diego, California, was named the greenest or most environmentally sustainable city in the United States, according to an annual study by personal finance company WalletHub. The ranking is based on two dozen criteria, from greenhouse gas emissions to open space and urban agriculture. Experts say that the area's diverse terrain and the rich biodiversity that it supports make San Diego an innovative space for environmental ideas and action."

Summary: San Diego, California, was named the greenest city in the U.S. by WalletHub due to its strong environmental performance, supported by diverse terrain, rich biodiversity, and innovative sustainability efforts.

Now summarize the following article:

Article: "Tech giant HomeTech unveiled its latest smart home hub, the 'Future Hub 10,' at a highly anticipated event in Silicon Valley this morning. The device boasts support for the Matter smart home standard and is compatible with both Amazon Alexa and Google Home devices. Pre-orders begin next month, with the official launch scheduled for Q4. Pricing is expected to be under $200."

Yes, few-shot prompts are often this lengthy and complex.

Here's another example. Let's say you work for a marketing firm, and you want AI to create a new blog post for a particular client. You can use the following few-shot prompt to provide the necessary background information to the AI model:

Task: Generate a blog post for our client, [CLIENT NAME]. Here is some information about the client:
[CLIENT DESCRIPTION]

**Here are some previous blog posts we've created for the client:**

**Example 1**
**Topic: [TOPIC]**
**Blog post: [BLOG POST CONTENT]**

**Example 2**
**Topic: [TOPIC]**
**Blog post: [BLOG POST CONTENT]**

**Write a 1,000-word blog post about [NEW TOPIC].**

Fill in everything in brackets with the actual content and you have a very specific few-shot prompt that should generate the relevant blog post you're looking for.

> **NOTE**   Unlike with one-shot prompting, few-shot prompting does not work with references to web pages or uploaded files. You must include your examples within the text of the prompt. (You could, however, extract examples from a web page or file and copy them into the prompt.)

# Best Practices for Effective Few-Shot Prompts

While few-shot prompting can improve AI results, doing it correctly can be challenging. With that in mind, follow these best practices for creating effective few-shot prompts:

- Use examples that are as similar as possible to your actual input.
- Make your examples different enough from each other to show the AI model multiple possible variations it might encounter.
- If you require a specific style or tone, reflect that in your examples.
- Use consistent formatting across all examples and your new task/input.
- Apply clear labels for each element of the prompt, such as Input, Output, Text, Summary, Question, Answer, and the like.
- Use shorter examples, if possible, to reduce the overall length of the prompt.
- Include as many examples as you need to train the AI, but not so many as to be superfluous (the sweet spot for total number of examples is between two and five).
- Ensure that your examples don't contain any errors, or the AI model will think the errors are normal.

And, as with all AI prompts, make sure that your prompts are as clear and as detailed as possible. Never assume that the AI model knows what you mean.

# Advanced Few-Shot Prompting Strategies

Want to make your few-shot prompts more effective? Here are a few advanced strategies to consider.

If you want the AI model to assume a particular persona when crafting its output, combine few-shot with role-based prompting. Simply add the phrase **as a [persona]** to the end of your instructions and enter a role, type of individual, or specific person within the brackets. For example, you might instruct the AI to answer a question **as a fourth-grade teacher**.

> **NOTE** Learn about role-based prompting in Chapter 9, "Using Role-Based Prompting."

If you want the AI model to mirror specific thinking, as with chain-of-thought prompting, include the reasoning steps that lead from the input to the output of each example. You do this by adding a "Reasoning" section between the example's input and output steps, as in the following example:

**Question: Ellie has 4 apples, then buys 3 more. She eats 2 apples. How many apples does she have left?**

**Reasoning: Ellie starts with 4 apples. She buys 3 more, so 4 + 3 = 7 apples. She eats 2 apples, so 7 - 2 = 5 apples.**

**Answer: 5 apples**

> **NOTE** Learn about chain-of-thought prompting in Chapter 10, "Using Chain-of-Thought Prompting."

You can sometimes achieve better results by employing self-consistency techniques to your few-shot prompts—that is, you prompt the AI multiple times, typically with slight variations in the prompts, to generate several sets of outputs. You then choose the output that is best or most consistent.

> **NOTE** Learn about self-consistency prompting in Chapter 11, "Using Self-Consistency Prompting."

Similarly, you can use iterative prompting to refine your few-shot results over a series of refined prompts. It's all about making the AI better with time and experience.

**NOTE**    Learn about iterative prompts in Chapter 15, "Refining Your Prompts."

# Limitations of Few-Shot Prompting

Few-shot prompting is a powerful technique, but it's not without its drawbacks and limitations. Take note of the following:

- AI performance is highly dependent on the quality of the examples used; poor or confusing examples can result in poor results.

- If the examples are too similar to each other, the AI model might "overfit" to those examples and not perform well on inputs that deviate from those examples.

- If the examples are too different from each other, the AI model may get confused and produce unpredictable results.

- If the input variables differ too much from the examples in a prompt, the AI model may struggle to provide acceptable results.

- The order of the examples within a prompt can sometimes affect the quality of the output.

- Any biases inherent in the examples may be reproduced in the AI output.

- The longer prompts inherent with few-shot prompting might be too lengthy or complex for some AI models to process.

- The more examples used, the more computational power used by the AI model, which can lead to slower execution times.

Keep these potential issues in mind if you choose to employ the few-shot prompting strategy.

**NOTE**    Because of these and other limitations, some experts frown on the use of few-shot prompting. This is particularly so with AI tools that combine data from large language models with results from traditional web searches. One such tool, Perplexity, explicitly advises users to avoid few-shot prompting, saying that it can trigger searches for the examples rather than the actual query.

## COMPARING FEW-SHOT AND OTHER SHOT-BASED PROMPTING STRATEGIES

As you've learned, the three shot-based prompting strategies differ primarily in how many examples are included or referenced in the prompt. Zero-shot prompting uses zero examples, one-shot prompting uses one example, and few-shot prompting uses two or more examples.

Because no examples are required, zero-shot prompting is better-suited for simpler tasks and less experienced users. It often produces less-predictable results, however, especially when specific output is required.

One-shot prompting is slightly more complex than zero-shot prompting but produced more predictable results. It's a good choice if you know the desired output or require a specific output style.

Few-shot prompting is the strategy to employ if one-shot prompting doesn't provide the desired style or content of results. By providing more than one example, you give the AI model more to work with, generating more predictable results.

In short, use zero-shot prompting for most tasks, one-shot for more demanding tasks, and few-shot for tasks that require the most specific output.

## Summary

In this chapter, you learned all about few-shot prompting, the prompting strategy that employs two or more examples within the prompt. You learned how few-shot works and how it compares to zero-shot and one-shot prompting. You learned when to use the few-shot strategy and best practices for crafting few-shot prompts.

Shot-based prompting is just one approach to crafting AI prompts, however. The next chapter covers a completely different approach to crafting AI instructions—role-based prompting.

9

# USING ROLE-BASED PROMPTING

In the previous three chapters, I discussed shot-based prompting strategies: zero-shot (with no examples), one-shot (with one example), and few-shot (with multiple examples). Now, it's time to move past prompts with examples to prompts that take on the persona of a given person or profession.

This approach is called role-based prompting, and it works by assigning AI a role or persona to shape the content, tone, and style of its output.

# What Role-Based Prompting Is and How It Works

Role-based prompting is the strategy of assigning a specific role or persona to the AI within your prompt. The rest of the prompt is essentially the same as what you'd do otherwise to describe the desired task and output; you just tell the AI what point of view to assume in crafting its output. This helps the AI deliver more relevant and targeted results—in a more realistic voice.

Role assignation is a simple addition to any type of AI prompt. While most role-based instructions are added onto zero-shot prompts, you can also use this strategy with one-shot and few-shot prompts. It's a simple matter of describing your task and output as normal and then adding on the role you want AI to assume. You can do this by adding **like a [ROLE]** to the end of a prompt. This simple addition tells the AI to approach the task like the assigned persona and craft its results accordingly—at the right grade level, level of knowledge, tone of voice, and so on.

You can assign AI any number of roles. You might, for example, tell AI to explain something "like an elementary school teacher," "like an electrician," "like a doctor," and so forth. For example, if you want an AI model to summarize a contract like a law professor, you'd enter the prompt:

**summarize the following contract like a law professor**

You can even have it assume the role of a real person or fictional character. For example, if you wanted AI to find the answer to a problem in the logical manner of fictional detective Sherlock Holmes, you'd enter the prompt:

**explain the solution like Sherlock Holmes**

The AI model then responds with the knowledge and voice of the persona or character selected.

Role-based prompting works because, in its vast database of information, AI has prior knowledge of the role or character you assign. The AI then uses what it knows about this persona to interpret how it should speak, what it should focus on, and what level and type of content to include. It will shift the language and tone used based on the persona; for example, a professor will use academic phrasing while a salesperson will speak more persuasively.

When you employ role-based prompting, you get results that are more relevant to your intended audience. The AI filters out information that isn't relevant and presents what is relevant in an accessible manner.

# When to Use Role-Based Prompting

Role-based prompting can be used in all manner of situations. It's best employed when you need to target the response to a specific audience and resonate with that audience.

Here are specific instances where role-based prompting makes particular sense:

- When the task requires specific insight or knowledge. For example, you should use role-based prompting when you need professional knowledge, such as tasks regarding legal, medical, or technical issues.

- When you need to tailor the tone and style to a specific audience. For example, you would use role-based prompting to establish the proper tone when you're writing for children, serious hobbyists, business professionals, and the like.

- When you want to simulate real-world scenarios, such as conversations, interviews, or interactive training. In essence, you instruct the AI to play a character in the scenario.

- When you're using AI in creative work, such as generating storylines or outlines, writing fiction, or brainstorming ideas.

- When you need to ensure consistency across multiple outputs, such as when you're writing a series of blog posts, articles, or support documents.

In short, you should use role-based prompting when you want to communicate clearly to a given audience in a specific tone or voice. Assign a given role to have AI simulate a person in that role.

# How to Craft a Role-Based Prompt

There are several ways you can craft a role-based prompt. The first is to add the role at the end of the prompt, using the following format:

**[PROMPT] like a [ROLE]**

So, for example, if you wanted AI to explain a given topic like an eighth-grade teacher, you'd craft a prompt like this one:

**explain nuclear fusion like an eighth-grade teacher**

Figure 9.1 shows how Google Gemini handles this prompt.

> ◆ Alright, everyone, let's talk about something that's super cool and powerful—so powerful, it's what makes our sun and all the other stars in the universe shine! It's called nuclear fusion.
>
> You've probably heard of nuclear fission, which is what's used in power plants and atomic bombs. That's when you take a big, heavy atom, like uranium, and you split it apart. Nuclear fusion is basically the opposite of that.
>
> **The Big Idea: Tiny Atoms, Big Energy**
>
> Imagine you have two tiny, lightweight atoms. We're talking about isotopes of hydrogen, the simplest element. Let's call them **deuterium** and **tritium**. They're like little balls of positive charge, so they naturally want to push each other away.
>
> Now, imagine we can smash them together with incredible force. To do this, we need to get them moving super fast. How do we do that? By making them incredibly, ridiculously hot—even hotter than the center of the sun! We're talking about temperatures over 100 million degrees Celsius.

**FIGURE 9.1**

*Google Gemini, assuming the role of an eighth-grade teacher.*

The second approach is to define the role up front, perhaps also with a description of the audience. That type of prompt would look like this:

**You are a [ROLE]. [PROMPT]**

In this instance, you put the task after the role definition. For example, if you want to have AI take the role of an auto mechanic, explaining how often to change the oil in your car, you'd craft a prompt like this one:

**You are a mechanic explaining how often to change the oil in a car.**

Figure 9.2 shows how ChatGPT responds to this request.

> Alright, here's the deal — I'm a mechanic, and I'm gonna keep this simple so you don't have to guess and blow your engine.
>
> **How often should you change your oil?**
> That depends on your car, your oil, and how you drive.
>
> **1. Check the owner's manual first.**
>
> Every car is different. Some newer cars can go **7,500 to 10,000 miles** between oil changes if they use **synthetic oil**. Older cars or ones using **conventional oil** usually need it every **3,000 to 5,000 miles.**
>
> **2. Look at your driving habits.**
>
> - If you're always stuck in traffic, taking short trips, driving in extreme heat or cold, or towing — change your oil **more often**. That's considered "severe driving."
> - If you're just cruising easy and not putting much strain on the engine, you can go a little longer. ↓

**FIGURE 9.2**

*ChatGPT, assuming the role of an auto mechanic.*

You could also use the following structure:

**Assume you are a [ROLE]. [PROMPT]**

Or:

**Assume the role of a [ROLE]. [PROMPT]**

Consider the following prompt, and (in Figure 9.3) how Meta AI responds:

**Assume you are a professional Cajun chef. Create an easy recipe for shrimp etouffee.**

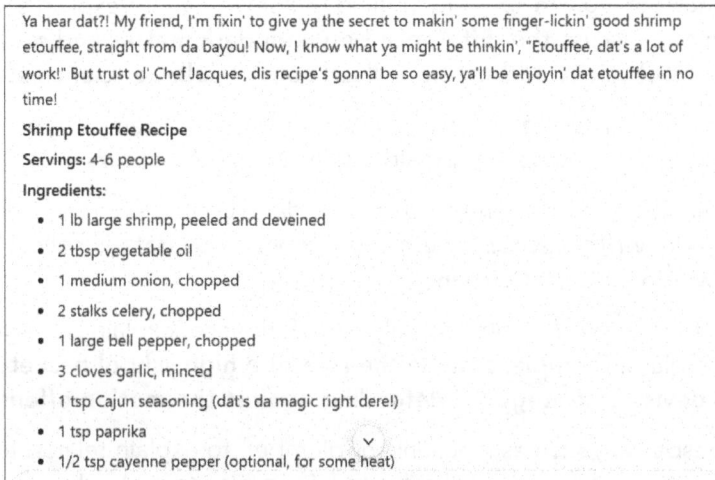

Ya hear dat?! My friend, I'm fixin' to give ya the secret to makin' some finger-lickin' good shrimp etouffee, straight from da bayou! Now, I know what ya might be thinkin', "Etouffee, dat's a lot of work!" But trust ol' Chef Jacques, dis recipe's gonna be so easy, ya'll be enjoyin' dat etouffee in no time!

**Shrimp Etouffee Recipe**

**Servings: 4-6 people**

**Ingredients:**

- 1 lb large shrimp, peeled and deveined
- 2 tbsp vegetable oil
- 1 medium onion, chopped
- 2 stalks celery, chopped
- 1 large bell pepper, chopped
- 3 cloves garlic, minced
- 1 tsp Cajun seasoning (dat's da magic right dere!)
- 1 tsp paprika
- 1/2 tsp cayenne pepper (optional, for some heat)

**FIGURE 9.3**

*MetaAI, assuming the role of a Cajun chef.*

# What Kinds of Roles Can You Have AI Assume?

With role-based prompting, you can have an AI model assume just about any role or persona you can think of. AI can become a subject matter expert, industry professional, educator, critic, and more. It can even become a struggling novelist or standup comic!

## Expert Roles

Some of the most common personas used in role-based prompting are those of subject-matter experts. Assign expert roles when topic-specific knowledge is required.

Some examples of expert roles include

- Doctor, nurse, or medical specialist for diagnosing symptoms, explaining medical conditions, recommending treatment plans, and other health-related tasks. Example: **assume the role of a general physician and explain treatment options for type 2 diabetes**

- Lawyer or legal advisor for interpreting laws, summarizing contracts, devising legal strategies, and other legal tasks. Example: **explain the benefits of trusts like an estate lawyer**

- Scientist, in a given specialty or field of knowledge, to explain scientific topics. Example: **discuss the difference between dark matter and dark energy as an astrophysicist addressing a classroom of college science students**

- Historian, to provide historical context or analysis. Example: **you are a historian ranking the top ten presidents of the 20th century**

- Statistician or data scientist, to analyze data, determine trends, and so on. Example: **write a scholarly essay on how census data is collected, as a knowledgeable statistician**

- Coach, for a given sport, to analyze performance, explain strategy, and recommend plays. Example: **assume the role of a high school basketball coach and devise a strategy for defending against the motion offense**

- Tradesperson, such as mechanic or plumber, to explain related topics, analyze problems, and recommend solutions. Example: **as a plumber, explain the pros and cons of copper and plastic pipes**

- Chef or cook, to create recipes and provide cooking advice. Example: **as a professional chef, explain the benefits of using fresh vs. frozen vegetables**

- Software engineer or developer, to help with coding and debugging, recommend best practices, or write code. Example: **act as a software developer and write HTML code for a website opt-out form**

## Educator Roles

Another popular persona for role-based prompting is that of an educator. This is effective when you need to explain or summarize a topic; it's also good for skill-building.

**NOTE**  It's not enough just to say, "like a teacher." You need to specify what type of teacher—grade level, topic, and so on.

For example, you can assign the role of

- Elementary school teacher (or specify precise grade). Example: **explain the difference between vowels and consonants like a second-grade teacher**

- Middle school teacher. Example: **discuss the causes of WWI like a middle school social studies teacher**

- High school teacher. Example: **you are a high school teacher and must create a curriculum for an introductory economics course**

- Teacher of a specific topic, such as a social studies teacher or an algebra teacher. Example: **explain the Pythagorean theorem like a geometry teacher**

- College professor (of a specific topic). Example: **you are a college philosophy professor summarizing the Hegelian Dialectic**

- Language coach (of a specific language). Example: **assume the role of a Spanish teacher and prepare a test to assess basic language knowledge**

- Workshop leader (for step-by-step lessons or skill training). Example: **for an upcoming workshop on municipal recycling, prepare a step-by-step lesson plan as if you were the workshop leader**

## Creative and Communication Roles

You can also assign AI a variety of creative and communications-related roles. This approach is useful when you're creating both fiction and nonfiction content.

You can assign any of the following roles:

- Writer, defined by genre, such as "mystery writer" or "cookbook writer." Example: **write a guide for changing oil in your lawn mower like a how-to writer**

- Novelist, for writing long-form fiction. Example: **assume the role of a novelist and generate an outline for a mystery novel based on the Lindbergh kidnapping**

- Poet; can be defined by genre. Example: **analyze Robert Frost's poem, "The Road Not Taken," like a poet**

- Screenwriter, for creating scripts, dialog, outlines, and the like; can be defined by genre. Example: **you are a screenwriter and must create a proposal for a television comedy series about three sisters living with their stepmother in a quirky small town**

- Blogger. Example: **as a blogger, determine how often we should post content to our company blog**

- Social media influencer. Example: **write a series of posts about the latest fall fashions like a social media influencer**

- Journalist, for factual reporting, interviews, or feature writing. Example: **write an article about the upcoming NFL draft like a sports journalist**

- Marketing copywriter, for writing persuasive ad and online copy. Example: **assume the role of a marketing copywriter and create an email promoting the grand opening of a new trampoline park**

## Strategic Roles

When you want AI to provide direction or help develop a strategy, you can assign AI a strategic role. This is useful when you need to brainstorm ideas, develop business or marketing plans, or make important decisions.

For example, you can assign the following strategic roles:

- Startup founder or entrepreneur, for brainstorming new business ideas. Example: **think like an entrepreneur and come up with five ideas for new businesses that take advantage of generative AI**

- CEO or other senior manager, for developing business plans and making important business decisions. Example: **You are the CEO of a mid-sized technology company facing declining customer retention. Analyze the situation and propose a high-level strategic plan to improve retention, focusing on customer experience and new product development.**

- Marketing strategist, for generating campaign and branding ideas, as well as creating marketing plans. Example: **Assume the role of a marketing strategist working for a local bridal shop. Create a marketing campaign targeted at older brides.**

- Business consultant, for providing advice to business owners and managers. Example: **As a business consultant, how would you advise dealing with an high-value employee who is being wooed by a competing company?**

- Project manager, for creating task lists and timelines, as well as managing workflow. Example: **You are the project manager for a construction project that involves tearing down an existing community center facility and building a new building, playground, and splash pad. Develop a timeline for the project, from start to finish.**

- Life coach or therapist, for emotional support, life planning, and so on. Example: **assume the role of a life coach and advise me whether I should continue in my current job or explore new career opportunities**

## Evaluator and Critic Roles

Assigning AI the role of an evaluator or critic can help you assess and critique content and situations. For example, you can assign the roles of

- Editor, to assess the grammar, structure, and content of a piece. Example: **review the attached article like an editor.**

- Proofreader, to find and correct spelling, punctuation, and formatting errors. Example: **assume the role of a proofreader and proofread the following blog post.**

- Literary critic, to review and evaluate works of fiction, essays, and the like. **You are the literary critic for a scholarly journal. Review the attached short story.**

- Academic or peer reviewer, to review and critique academic papers. Example: **critique the attached paper as a peer reviewer.**

- Product reviewer, to review and compare consumer products. Example: **Pretend that you're a professional product reviewer and provide a review of the latest television [MODEL] from [COMPANY].**

- Legal advisor or contract reviewer, to evaluate contracts and other documents for regulatory compliance, legal risk, and clarity. Example: **As the company's legal advisor, review the attached contract for regulatory and legal compliance.**

- Financial analyst, to assess budgets, forecasts, and investment opportunities for accuracy and viability. Example: **Act as my financial advisor and recommend five index funds with a mix of low-risk and long-term potential.**

## Fictional and Real-Life Roles

Finally, you can instruct AI models to approach a task like a given person might. That person might be real or might be fictional. This is useful when you want your output to reflect the tone of that individual—to sound like a person but address the task at hand. You can use this approach for both instructional and creative content.

Here are some examples:

- **Explain how gravity works like Neil DeGrasse Tyson.**
- **Write a poem about winter in the style of Edgar Allen Poe.**
- **Give me a five-minute comedy routine about high school in the style of Nate Bargatze.**
- **You are Oprah Winfrey. Provide uplifting advice for someone going through a major life transition.**
- **As Vince Lombardi, provide some advice to our high school football team.**
- **Describe how to cook a turkey in the style of Stephen King.**
- **You are Master Yoda. Teach me how to stay calm and focused during stressful work situations.**
- **Analyze the current Senate race like James Carville.**

You get the idea. You can have some real fun with this one. (Figure 9.4 shows what happens when you ask Claude to explain fly fishing like hardboiled fictional detective Philip Marlow; fun stuff.)

> The sun was setting over the river like a cheap suit on a drunk, all wrinkled and ready to hit the gutter. I stood there with a nine-foot rod in my hands, feeling about as useful as a screen door on a submarine. Fly fishing, they called it. Sounded innocent enough, like something your maiden aunt might take up after bridge club got too exciting.
>
> But this game had more angles than a crooked politician's alibi.
>
> First thing you learn is that the fly isn't a fly at all - it's a lie dressed up in feathers and thread, designed to fool something with a brain the size of a pea. The irony wasn't lost on me. In my line of work, I was used to people lying to fish for information. Here, I was lying to fish for fish.
>
> The rod becomes an extension of your arm, like a .38 becomes an extension of your will. You learn to read the water the way you read a suspect's face - looking for the tells, the shadows, the places where something might be hiding. The trout are down there somewhere, cold and calculating as loan sharks, waiting for the right opportunity to strike.
>
> Casting is where the poetry meets the pavement. It's all about timing and rhythm, like a good interrogation. Too eager and you spook your target. Too slow and the moment passes you by. You whip that line back and forth through the air, watching it unfurl like smoke from a Camel, hoping it lands where you meant it to and not wrapped around your neck like a silk tie with homicidal intentions.

**FIGURE 9.4**

*Claude explaining fly fishing like Philip Marlowe would.*

# Best Practices for Effective Role-Based Prompts

When you want to achieve the best results from role-based prompting, follow these best practices:

- **Assign an easily understood role:** The more obscure the role, the less likely it is that the AI model will know enough about it.

- **Clearly define the rule:** Ambiguous instructions can lead to generic answers or output that is way off target.

- **Set the relevant scenario within the prompt:** Provide appropriate context to the role (such as "airplane pilot giving a preflight briefing").

- **Specify the audience:** A teacher speaking to an audience of 12-year-olds will use a different approach than when speaking to their parents.

- **Experiment with similar but slightly different roles:** For example, the roles of "writer," "author," "journalist," and "blogger" will produce subtly different results.

- **When chaining prompts, stay in character:** Use the same persona when crafting multiple related prompts.

> **NOTE**  Learn more about how to chain prompts in Chapter 12, "Using Prompt Chaining."

As always, the rest of your prompt should include as many details as necessary. You also need to clearly define the output format. And remember to test your role-based prompts—and revise them if the results aren't quite as you expected.

# Advanced Role-Based Prompting Strategies

How can you get better results from role-based prompting? Here are some advanced strategies to employ:

- Combine role-based prompting with other prompting approaches to generate results with the style and knowledge of a given individual or occupation. For example, you can assign AI the role of a physician and have it work step-by-step through a given diagnosis using a chain-of-thought prompt, like this: **Assume the role of a physician and diagnose a persistent cough, presenting all your steps.**

- Add detail to a role by providing a specific experience level, worldview, or ideology. This helps you fine-tune a given role. For example, instead of assigning the role of **farmer**, describe the role as an **organic farmer on a**

**small family farm**. You can also give the AI a distinct personality or detailed backstory to help better direct the desired output.

- Assign the AI multiple roles to combine skills or perspectives. This is called multi-hat prompting and can provide results more akin to those of a team than an individual. Take the following prompt as an example of combining roles: **You are an application developer and copywriter working together as a team. Create consumer documentation for a new mental health app.**

- Switch roles in mid-conversation to simulate an interview or debate. This is called multi-turn roleplay, and you use it within an ongoing conversation with an AI model. Start by assigning the AI its initial role, then at some point, tell it to assume a different role. For example, you could have the AI assume the role of an entrepreneur pitching a new idea, then switch gears and have the AI become a skeptical investor being given the pitch.

# Limitations of Role-Based Prompting

Role-based prompting can be extremely useful and a little fun, but it does have its limitations. It isn't good for every situation, and there are some things you need to be cautious about.

First, know that AI can only mimic a given role based on patterns in its training data. AI doesn't actually understand the role or possess real-world experience, which means its output might be superficial. For example, an AI "doctor" may sound like an expert but lack the clinical judgment of a real physician. You should not take the advice given by an AI model as authoritative; always fact-check any advice you receive.

Similarly, since AI relies on existing data to construct its assigned persona, it may pick up bad habits and biases. It can also fall into easy stereotypes and provide overly clichéd responses. It's not a real person, remember, just an image of one.

Next, know that AI models can easily get confused, especially if you combine multiple roles in a prompt. It might sound like a good idea to have AI function as both a corporate lawyer and a kindergarten teacher, but that conflicting prompt is likely to yield a confusing output.

If you're carrying on a long conversation with a role-based AI model, look out for what experts call "role drift." This happens when an AI model drifts out of its original role after several follow-on prompts. You can avoid this by occasionally reminding the AI of its assigned role.

Finally, you shouldn't rely on AI—even role-based AI—for important decisions. An AI model is not a real doctor, lawyer, or therapist. When there's something important on the table, ditch the AI and go right to a real professional.

## COMPARING ROLE-BASED PROMPTING TO OTHER PROMPTING STRATEGIES

Role-based prompting is an easy way to get specific types of output from an AI model. Other prompting strategies might be better suited for some tasks, however.

Compared to zero-shot prompting, role-based prompting is slightly more complete; it forces you to think about a given role and describe that role to the AI model. That said, assigning a role to a zero-shot prompt is a good way to add more depth and a more precise tone to the AI results.

Role-based prompting is not necessarily a good substitute for one- or few-shot prompting, however. If you're providing one or more examples in your prompt, you don't need to also assign a role to the AI; all necessary information should be in the examples.

Role-based prompting is also not a good substitute for chain-of-thought or self-consistency prompting, although it can supplement both of those approaches. Adding a role to a chain-of-thought prompt will let you see how a given persona "thinks," and blending self-consistency and role-based prompting gives you several options based on the assigned persona.

In short, role-based prompting is a good way to provide direction to most other types of prompts, one- and few-shot prompting excepted. Try it to see what you get.

## Summary

In this chapter, you learned all about role-based prompting—what it is, how it works, and how and when to use it. Role-based prompting is a very powerful strategy for instructing AI models, and one you should be using on a regular basis.

Next up, a totally different approach to AI prompting: the chain-of-thought strategy.

# 10

# USING CHAIN-OF-THOUGHT PROMPTING

Oftentimes, you prompt AI and only want a simple answer. Other times, however, it may be useful to understand exactly how an AI model figured out its result. When you need to know the thinking behind the AI, you need to use chain-of-thought prompting.

Instead of just providing a final answer, chain-of-thought prompting directs the AI to break down its reasoning into a series of intermediate steps. You're instructing the AI to show its work, which is useful when you're working with complex math or reasoning problems.

# What Chain-of-Thought Prompting Is and How It Works

Most people view AI as kind of a magic box. You ask it to do something (the prompt), your request goes into the magic AI box, and then you get the answer or output on the other side. You don't know or particularly care what happens in the middle; it all happens out of sight and behind the scenes.

That's fine for a lot of tasks where you really don't need to know how AI came up with its results. All you need is the answer or generated content, and what happens in the magic box doesn't matter to you.

There are other times, however, when it may be useful to see the steps that AI took to answer your question. Knowing the steps that AI took to get to the solution can help you better understand the problem or task at hand, as well as identify any flaws in the AI's logic.

That's where chain-of-thought prompting comes in. Chain-of-thought prompting is a way of instructing an AI model to show the reasoning steps it works through when it's solving a problem or answering a question. Instead of showing you only the final answer, the AI walks through its reasoning step-by-step, kind of like a student showing their work on a math problem.

In addition, some AI models actually perform better with reasoning tasks when they're instructed to generate these intermediate steps. It forces them to lean into their pattern recognition capabilities by mimicking how humans naturally think through such problems.

Initiating a chain-of-thought prompt is as simple as adding to your prompt something like "show your thinking step by step" or even just "step -by step." That's enough to let the AI model know that it needs to show all the steps of its reasoning in its results.

# When to Use Chain-of-Thought Prompting

Chain-of-thought prompting is not practical for all types of tasks. If you just want a simple answer to a simple question, you don't need the AI to show its steps. (In fact, it probably doesn't have any steps if reasoning is not required.) You also don't need to use chain-of-thought prompting when you're generating specific types of creative output, such as reports, blog posts, translations, outlines, and the like.

Where the chain-of-thought prompting strategy shines is with tasks that require logic and reasoning. If the AI model needs to "think through" a task, you can use chain-of-thought prompting to have it show you the steps it is taking.

So, consider using chain-of-thought prompting for the following types of tasks:

- Math problems, especially word problems
- Tasks that require combining information or results from multiple prompts or sources of information (called *multi-hop* prompts)
- Tasks where a conclusion must be derived via logical reasoning or deduction from a set of facts or rules
- Questions where the answer must be derived from real-world knowledge
- Planning or decision-making when the AI model needs to weigh options and predict outcomes

For example, the following math word problem is an ideal candidate for chain-of-thought prompting:

**Sandy has 5 boxes. Each box contains 10 pencils. She gives away 12 pencils to her friends. How many pencils does she have left? Show your work.**

Figure 10.1 shows the reasoning steps taken by ChatGPT in solving this problem.

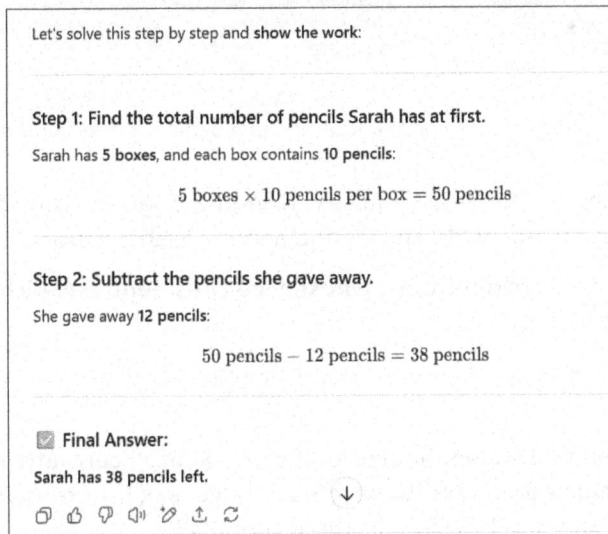

> Let's solve this step by step and **show the work:**
>
> **Step 1: Find the total number of pencils Sarah has at first.**
>
> Sarah has **5 boxes**, and each box contains **10 pencils**:
>
> $$5 \text{ boxes} \times 10 \text{ pencils per box} = 50 \text{ pencils}$$
>
> **Step 2: Subtract the pencils she gave away.**
>
> She gave away **12 pencils**:
>
> $$50 \text{ pencils} - 12 \text{ pencils} = 38 \text{ pencils}$$
>
> ☑ **Final Answer:**
>
> Sarah has **38 pencils left.**

**FIGURE 10.1**

*Chain-of-thought reasoning from ChatGPT for a math problem.*

Here's another example, where the AI model must consider a series of statements and deduce the proper answer:

**If all bears are mammals, and some mammals can swim, can we conclude that all bears can swim? Provide step-by-step reasoning.**

Figure 10.2 shows the start of Google Gemini's step-by-step reasoning to this question.

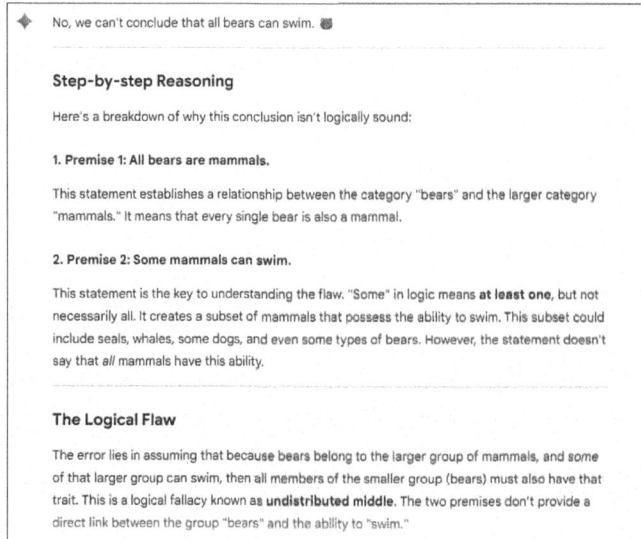

No, we can't conclude that all bears can swim. 🐻

**Step-by-step Reasoning**

Here's a breakdown of why this conclusion isn't logically sound:

**1. Premise 1: All bears are mammals.**

This statement establishes a relationship between the category "bears" and the larger category "mammals." It means that every single bear is also a mammal.

**2. Premise 2: Some mammals can swim.**

This statement is the key to understanding the flaw. "Some" in logic means **at least one**, but not necessarily all. It creates a subset of mammals that possess the ability to swim. This subset could include seals, whales, some dogs, and even some types of bears. However, the statement doesn't say that *all* mammals have this ability.

**The Logical Flaw**

The error lies in assuming that because bears belong to the larger group of mammals, and *some* of that larger group can swim, then all members of the smaller group (bears) must also have that trait. This is a logical fallacy known as **undistributed middle**. The two premises don't provide a direct link between the group "bears" and the ability to "swim."

**FIGURE 10.2**

*Google Gemini working through the logical steps behind a chain-of-thought prompt.*

The next example shows how AI uses chain-of-thought thinking to derive an answer based on real-world knowledge and multi-hop reasoning.

**Where was the president born whose vice president was Richard Nixon? Show step by step.**

And here's an example of how chain-of-thought prompting can help you plan a budget:

**I want to buy a new electric bike that costs $950. I currently have $200 in the bank. How much do I need to save each paycheck if I get paid twice a month and want to buy the bike within three months?**

ChatGPT walks you through the steps in Figure 10.3.

Let's walk through this step by step **logically** to figure out how much you need to save each paycheck.

**Step 1: Determine how much you still need to save.**

You want to buy an electric bike that costs **$950**, and you already have **$200** in the bank.

$$\$950 - \$200 = \$750$$

So, you still need to save **$750**.

**Step 2: Calculate how many paychecks you'll get in 3 months.**

You get paid **twice a month**, so over 3 months, you'll receive:

$$2 \text{ paychecks/month} \times 3 \text{ months} = 6 \text{ paychecks}$$

**Step 3: Divide the amount you need to save by the number of paychecks.**

$$\$750 \div 6 = \$125$$

☑ **Final Answer:**

You need to save **$125 from each paycheck** for the next 6 paychecks to afford the $950 electric bike in 3 months.

**FIGURE 10.3**

*Walking through the steps of a budget plan, thanks to ChatGPT.*

**NOTE**  Chain-of-thought prompting results in very detailed, very thoughtful results. If all you need is the answer or when brevity is essential, this isn't the approach to take.

# How to Craft a Chain-of-Thought Prompt

There are two ways to craft a chain-of-thought prompt.

The first approach is to ask the AI model to "show your steps," "think step-by-step," or "think logically" by adding those words to the end of the prompt. For example, if you wanted to know how many days it would take to drive from Texas to Oregon, you could use the prompt:

**Driving 8 hours a day, how many days does it take to drive from Dallas to Seattle? Think step by step.**

You can also combine chain-of-thought with few-shot prompting to provide the AI with examples of the step-by-step thinking you desire, as in the following example:

**Examples:**

**Q1: There are 2 dogs. Each has 3 puppies. How many puppies are there in total?**

**A1: Each dog has 3 puppies. 2 × 3 = 6 puppies.**

**Q2: There are 5 baskets. Each basket has 4 apples. How many apples are there in total?**

**A2: Each basket has 4 apples. 5 × 4 = 20 apples.**

**New question:**

**There are 3 cars, each holding 4 people. How many people are there in total?**

In most instances, however, the manual method is the easiest approach.

# Best Practices for Effective Chain-of-Thought Prompts

For the best results when using chain-of-thought prompting, follow these best practices:

- Clearly and explicitly instruct the AI to use step-by-step thinking. Don't assume the AI will always show its work.

- Structure your prompt to naturally lead the model through the problem. If the problem has several distinct parts, consider using number lists or bullet points within the prompt to organize the information. (You can also lead the AI via ordered text, such as "first," "second," and "third.")

- Use clear and unambiguous language. Avoid overly complex sentences, jargon, or ambiguous terms.

- For complex tasks, ask for the answer separately after the steps have been presented. Use a prompt like **what is the final answer?**

# Advanced Chain-of-Thought Prompting Strategies

There are several ways you can achieve even better results with chain-of-thought prompting, many involving combining chain-of-thought with other prompting strategies.

For example, if you want to reduce the risk of receiving inaccurate results, combine chain-of-thought with self-consistency prompting. All you have to do is enter the same prompt (or the same prompt with slight variations) multiple times, then compare the different results, and see how they approach the problem. Choose the solution that appears most frequently.

> **NOTE**    Learn more about self-consistency prompting in Chapter 11, "Using Self-Consistency Prompting."

Similarly, you can employ *tree-of-thought* prompting to generate multiple possibilities. Instead of asking for a single linear chain of reasoning, instruct the AI model to generate multiple potential reasoning paths, then evaluate the options and determine which path is most promising to pursue further. At each step of the process, ask the AI model to produce several different next steps ("thoughts") and then prompt the model to evaluate the quality of each thought. ("Which of these approaches is most likely to lead to the correct answer?") Choose the most promising path and keep going until the final solution is reached.

Finally, when you're dealing with extremely complex problems, consider breaking the problem down into a series of simpler subproblems. Task the AI model with solving the easier subproblems first and then use those solutions in new prompts to solve the more complex subproblems. Continue in this fashion until the original, complex problem is solved. (This is called *least-to-most prompting*.)

# Limitations of Chain-of-Thought Prompting

Chain-of-thought prompting is not without its issues, the first being that it isn't ideally suited for all types of AI-related tasks. You should also consider these additional limitations of the chain-of-thought model:

- Chain-of-thought prompting works best with large AI models. Models working with smaller amounts of data can sometimes struggle to produce coherent reasoning steps and may, in fact, produce worse results than standard zero-shot prompting.

- Chain-of-thought prompting requires more computational resources than other prompting strategies. If your access or resources are limited, you may want to choose a simpler prompting strategy.

- Because it's more complex, chain-of-thought prompting is also slower than other prompting strategies.

- If you use the chain-of-thought strategy for relatively simple requests, you may end up with a more verbose answer than is necessary.

- Chain-of-thought reasoning is highly sensitive to a prompt's wording and for-mat. The AI can be distracted by irrelevant information in the prompt or con-fused by the order of instructions. Changing the wording or order can result in wildly different results.

- Chain-of-thought reasoning isn't always correct. While a given reasoning string might seem logical, that doesn't mean that it is. As with all things AI, always fully scrutinize the results.

## COMPARING CHAIN-OF-THOUGHT WITH OTHER PROMPTING STRATEGIES

You should consider using chain-of-thought prompting in special cases only. It can overcomplicate simple tasks that are best achieved via zero-shot prompting and might not be necessary if you're using one- or few-shot prompting.

That said, chain-of-thought prompting is useful when you want to see the AI model's step-by-step reasoning. It can help you better understand how to get results, rather than just being presented with those results. It's certainly useful for specific types of math and logic problems that might not be suitable for other prompting strategies.

# Summary

In this chapter, you learned how to use chain-of-thought prompting to show the step-by-step thinking behind complex tasks. You learned when best to use chain-of-thought prompting, how to construct an effective chain-of-thought prompt, and how to use chain-of-thought with other prompting strategies.

Speaking of those other prompting strategies, I have one more strategy to share. Turn the page to learn all about self-consistency prompting—and how best to use it.

# 11

# USING SELF-CONSISTENCY PROMPTING

Most AI queries result in a single response; you essentially take the first answer you get and assume (or hope) it's correct. But AI doesn't always deliver accurate or even consistent results. You may ask the same question multiple times and get slightly varying results.

If you want to improve the reasoning accuracy of an AI engine, you can use the strategy known as self-consistency prompting. In this strategy, you ask the AI model to generate multiple reasoning paths, often by running the same prompt multiple times, and then select the most consistent results.

The result is a way to create a consensus answer to complex questions.

# What Self-Consistency Prompting Is and How It Works

All the prompting strategies up to this point deliver a single result based on a single reasoning path. That might be good enough for simple tasks, but some tasks can benefit from approaching the issue from varying angles, using multiple reasoning paths. That's where self-consistency prompting comes in.

Self-consistency prompting is a way to use multiple diverse reasoning paths to generate multiple answers. You (or the AI) then choose the most consistent answer, essentially arriving at the "best" result through a form of majority voting. The results that occur most often are judged to be the best, and thus the ones you should choose as your "final answer."

This strategy works by prompting the AI model multiple times—asking the same question but letting the AI model produce different reasoning chains with different degrees of randomness. This approach works best with chain-of-thought prompts, so you can see the reasoning used in each attempt.

**NOTE**    In AI parlance, randomness is referred to as *temperature*. The more random the prompts and reasoning, the higher the temperature.

The AI model then collects all the results, all arrived at with their own reasoning, and compares the final answers from each reasoning chain. AI arrives at its "final" answer by picking the most consistent answer—the results that appear most often across all reasoning chains. It's this most common answer that is statistically most likely to be correct.

# When to Use Self-Consistency Prompting

Why might you want to use self-consistency prompting? There are several reasons.

First, self-consistency prompting reduces errors. AI isn't perfect, and a single approach to reasoning out a problem *could* result in an inaccurate recommendation. Running multiple reasoning paths helps to solidify the best reasoning and minimize the effect of a mistake in any given path.

Second, self-consistency prompting provides more diversity in reasoning. When the correct answer isn't obvious, this strategy works through enough options to determine the best approach.

Finally, self-consistency prompting provides you with more options to choose from. When you're dealing with a creative issue, such as generating an outline or writing an article, it's often good to have more options to choose from.

So, then, when should you use self-consistency prompting? Consider using this strategy for the following tasks:

- Complex math problems
- Complex logic problems
- Situations where accuracy is paramount
- Situations where you want a variety of creative options

# How to Craft a Self-Consistency Prompt

Crafting a self-consistency prompt is as simple as determining your base prompt and then adding instructions to create multiple reasoning paths. The base prompt can be any type of prompt—zero-shot, chain-of-thought, you name it. The key is to force the AI model to automatically run the prompt multiple times, aggregate the results, and choose the most consistent result as the final answer.

You do this by prefacing the desired task with the following text:

**Given the following problem, generate multiple answers using diverse reasoning paths and aggregate the answers to come to a final conclusion.**

Enter this text, followed by the task or problem you want solved, and let the AI model do its thing.

For example, consider the following prompt:

**Given the following problem, generate multiple answers using diverse reasoning paths and aggregate the answers to come to a final conclusion.**

**Willow had 5 sweaters. If she threw away 2 old ones and bought 3 new ones, how many sweaters would she have?**

Figure 11.1 shows how Google Gemini approached the problem with multiple lines of reasoning.

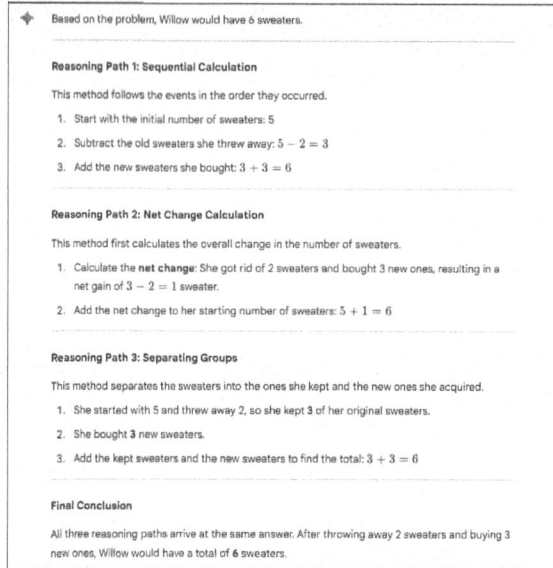

**FIGURE 11.1**

*Self-consistency prompting from Google Gemini.*

Here's another example of a problem that benefits from being analyzed in several different ways:

**Given the following problem, generate multiple answers using diverse reasoning paths and aggregate the answers to come to a final conclusion.**

**A man lies on the sand and looks up at the rocky cliffs. Where is the man?**

Figure 11.2 shows how Meta AI reasoned through the problem to come up with the most likely result.

You can also instruct the AI model as to how much to vary the reasoning paths. Simply introduce the following phrase and adjust the temperature accordingly:

**Use temperature [0.1 TO 1.0] to introduce variation.**

The higher the temperature, the more diverse the reasoning paths. The lower the temperature, the more similar the reasoning.

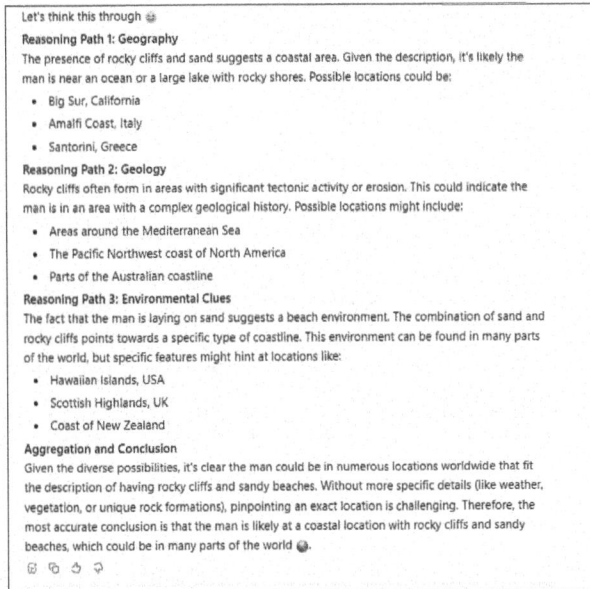

Let's think this through 😄
**Reasoning Path 1: Geography**
The presence of rocky cliffs and sand suggests a coastal area. Given the description, it's likely the man is near an ocean or a large lake with rocky shores. Possible locations could be:

- Big Sur, California
- Amalfi Coast, Italy
- Santorini, Greece

**Reasoning Path 2: Geology**
Rocky cliffs often form in areas with significant tectonic activity or erosion. This could indicate the man is in an area with a complex geological history. Possible locations might include:

- Areas around the Mediterranean Sea
- The Pacific Northwest coast of North America
- Parts of the Australian coastline

**Reasoning Path 3: Environmental Clues**
The fact that the man is laying on sand suggests a beach environment. The combination of sand and rocky cliffs points towards a specific type of coastline. This environment can be found in many parts of the world, but specific features might hint at locations like:

- Hawaiian Islands, USA
- Scottish Highlands, UK
- Coast of New Zealand

**Aggregation and Conclusion**
Given the diverse possibilities, it's clear the man could be in numerous locations worldwide that fit the description of having rocky cliffs and sandy beaches. Without more specific details (like weather, vegetation, or unique rock formations), pinpointing an exact location is challenging. Therefore, the most accurate conclusion is that the man is likely at a coastal location with rocky cliffs and sandy beaches, which could be in many parts of the world 😄.

## FIGURE 11.2

*Self-consistency prompting from Meta AI.*

Here's an example that requests a moderately high degree (0.7) of diversity:

**Given the following problem, generate multiple answers using diverse reasoning paths and aggregate the answers to come to a final conclusion. Use temperature 0.7 to introduce variation.**

**Rewrite the following sentence to improve clarity and impact:**

**Heidi hated the feeling of her emotions stacking onto itself, one after another, but sometimes it felt like she was just holding on for dear life; it made her feel like virtually everything in the world was completely out of her control.**

Figure 11.3 shows the different approaches that ChatGPT used, and Figure 11.4 shows ChatGPT's final recommendation.

Nice — I used a **moderately creative** approach (temperature ≈ **0.7**) and produced several distinct rewrites that explore different reasoning paths (clarity, concision, metaphor, rhythm, voice). Each option shows the approach, then the rewrite. At the end I summarize the common improvements and give a single recommended sentence.

### Rewrites

1. **Conservative / clarity** — *fix grammar, reduce redundancy, keep original voice*
   Heidi hated the way her emotions piled up, one after another. Sometimes she felt she was simply holding on for dear life, as if everything in her world had slipped beyond her control.

2. **Concise / punchy** — *shorter, higher impact*
   Heidi hated her emotions piling up. Sometimes she clung on for dear life, convinced the world had slipped from her grasp.

3. **Strong-verbs / tightened** — *swap weak phrasing for active verbs, tighten rhythm*
   Heidi loathed how her emotions stacked and pressed in; at times she clung to the moment, certain the rest of the world had slipped beyond her control.

4. **Metaphorical / sensory** — *one clear image to heighten feeling*
   Heidi hated how her emotions rose like a tide, wave after wave; sometimes she could only hang on, sure the current had pulled the world out of reach.

5. **Staccato / urgent** — *short fragments, more immediacy*
   Emotions stacking. One after another. Heidi hated it. Sometimes she hung on by her fingernails, convinced the world had spun out of her control.

6. **Lyrical / literary** — *elevated tone, compact image*
   Her feelings formed an unstable tower; Heidi hated the weight. Now and then she clung to its edge, convinced everything else had toppled beyond her reach.

7. **First-person / intimate** — *switch voice for immediacy and empathy*
   I hate the way my emotions pile up—one after another. Sometimes I hang on for dear life, convinced everything in my world is out of my control.

## FIGURE 11.3

*ChatGPT's various reasoning paths for a self-consistency prompt.*

### Aggregation & final recommendation

**What the variants agree on (key fixes):**

- Replace the awkward *"stacking onto itself"* with clearer verbs: *piled up, stacked, rose, formed.*
- Remove redundant qualifiers (*virtually / completely / it made her feel like*).
- Use one strong image or rhythm instead of multiple weak phrases.
- Prefer active verbs (*hated, loathed, clung*) for impact.

**Recommended final sentence (balanced clarity + impact):**
Heidi hated the way her emotions piled up, one after another; sometimes she could only cling on for dear life, convinced the world had slipped beyond her control.

Why this one? It fixes the clumsy phrasing, keeps the original meaning, tightens redundancy, and adds a single powerful image of clinging that preserves emotional urgency without overdoing the metaphor.

## FIGURE 11.4

*ChatGPT's final recommendation.*

**NOTE**    If you set the temperature too low, all the reasoning paths will be similar. It's better, at least early in the process, to use a higher temperature to generate more diversity in reasoning.

You can also use self-consistency prompting to generate and synthesize creative ideas. For example, here's a prompt for creating an outline for a college paper:

**Given the following task, generate multiple answers using diverse reasoning paths and aggregate the answers to come to a final conclusion. Use temperature 0.5 to introduce variation.**

**Generate an outline for a college paper on the effects of social media on news consumption.**

Figure 11.5 shows three of the five reasoning paths that Claude used to approach this task. Figure 11.6 shows the first part of Claude's suggested outline, incorporating insights from all the reasoning paths.

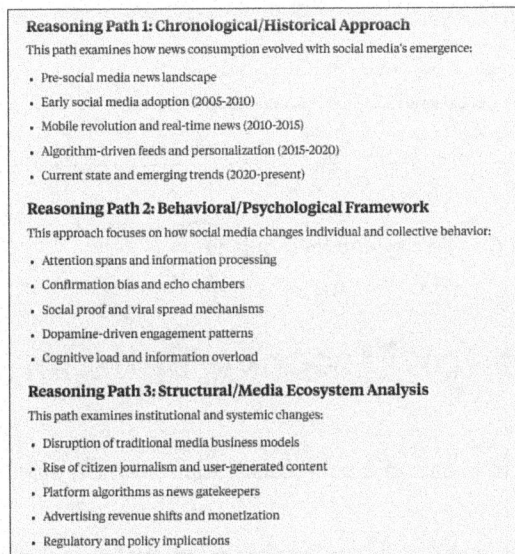

> **Reasoning Path 1: Chronological/Historical Approach**
>
> This path examines how news consumption evolved with social media's emergence:
>
> - Pre-social media news landscape
> - Early social media adoption (2005-2010)
> - Mobile revolution and real-time news (2010-2015)
> - Algorithm-driven feeds and personalization (2015-2020)
> - Current state and emerging trends (2020-present)
>
> **Reasoning Path 2: Behavioral/Psychological Framework**
>
> This approach focuses on how social media changes individual and collective behavior:
>
> - Attention spans and information processing
> - Confirmation bias and echo chambers
> - Social proof and viral spread mechanisms
> - Dopamine-driven engagement patterns
> - Cognitive load and information overload
>
> **Reasoning Path 3: Structural/Media Ecosystem Analysis**
>
> This path examines institutional and systemic changes:
>
> - Disruption of traditional media business models
> - Rise of citizen journalism and user-generated content
> - Platform algorithms as news gatekeepers
> - Advertising revenue shifts and monetization
> - Regulatory and policy implications

**FIGURE 11.5**

*The reasoning paths employed by Claude when creating an outline.*

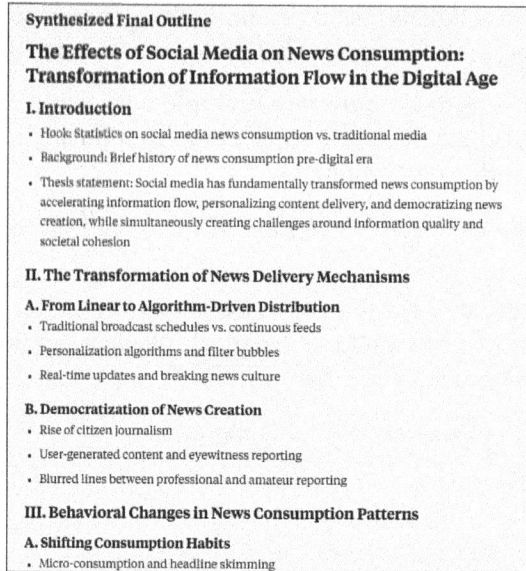

> **Synthesized Final Outline**
>
> **The Effects of Social Media on News Consumption: Transformation of Information Flow in the Digital Age**
>
> **I. Introduction**
> - Hook: Statistics on social media news consumption vs. traditional media
> - Background: Brief history of news consumption pre-digital era
> - Thesis statement: Social media has fundamentally transformed news consumption by accelerating information flow, personalizing content delivery, and democratizing news creation, while simultaneously creating challenges around information quality and societal cohesion
>
> **II. The Transformation of News Delivery Mechanisms**
>
> **A. From Linear to Algorithm-Driven Distribution**
> - Traditional broadcast schedules vs. continuous feeds
> - Personalization algorithms and filter bubbles
> - Real-time updates and breaking news culture
>
> **B. Democratization of News Creation**
> - Rise of citizen journalism
> - User-generated content and eyewitness reporting
> - Blurred lines between professional and amateur reporting
>
> **III. Behavioral Changes in News Consumption Patterns**
>
> **A. Shifting Consumption Habits**
> - Micro-consumption and headline skimming

**FIGURE 11.6**

The beginning of Claude's synthesized outline.

# Best Practices for Effective Self-Consistency Prompting

When it comes to creating a self-consistency prompt, adhere to the following best practices:

- Make sure that the task can benefit from evaluating multiple reasoning paths.
- Begin with a clear and concise base prompt.
- Clearly instruct the AI to provide multiple reasoning paths.
- Ask the AI to aggregate the results to provide a final answer.
- Use the optional temperature variable to determine how diverse the reasoning paths should be.

# Advanced Self-Consistency Prompting Strategies

There are several ways to superpower a self-consistency prompt. Consider the following advanced techniques:

- Specify an exact number of reasoning paths generated by the AI model. Use the text **generate [X] runs** or **generate [x] reasoning paths**, where X is the desired number of runs. More reasoning paths will introduce more diverse ideas, to a point.

- Instead of running all prompts with the same temperature (diversity level), use a multitemperature approach. Start with a higher temperature (0.9 to 1.0) to generate different reasoning paths, then rerun the most common answers at a lower temperature (0.1 to 0.3) to verify the answers with narrower variations.

- Use reasoning-path clustering to group responses by similar reasoning structure. Ask the AI to group responses by similar reasoning so you can weigh the reasoning diversity versus answer reasoning frequency when determining the best result.

- Have the AI model rate its confidence in each reasoning path and then weight votes by this confidence score. This will help identify better answers that might be generated with less frequency.

- Perform an answer reconciliation pass by feeding the top three responses back to the model and asking the AI to compare them, identify any flaws, and choose the most likely correct one.

To get superior results, go beyond simple multiple-run majority voting. Use these techniques to generate maximum diversity early in the process and then verify those results in later runs.

# Limitations of Self-Consistency Prompting

Self-consistency prompting is a more complex approach than other prompting strategies. As such, it is not without its limitations.

Consider first how many runs the AI model might make. If it makes too few runs, you get little improvement over the single chain-of-thought approach.

That said, once you get past a certain number of runs (typically about a dozen), generating additional reasoning paths rarely improves accuracy. That's why, without prompting, most AI models will generate a half-dozen or so runs; specifying a higher number of runs may result in diminishing returns.

Also consider the temperature used. A higher temperature will generate more diverse reasoning, where a lower temperature will create more similar, if not identical, reasoning paths. In general, more diversity is better.

It's also important to know that generating multiple reasoning paths can reinforce any inaccuracies or biases in the original prompt. If there's something wrong with the basic prompt, multiple runs are likely to repeat that error.

Self-consistency prompting can break down if you have an ambiguous task or one with multiple possible solutions. AI models often have problems when there's no "most correct" solution on which to converge.

In addition, self-consistency prompting won't always deliver the best answer. AI can recommend the wrong solution if a flawed reasoning path is somehow more appealing or if the correct path is less common. As with all things AI, don't take the recommended solution at face value; give everything a logic and fact check.

Finally, know that self-consistency prompting is more resource-intensive than other prompting strategies. Use this strategy gingerly if resources are at a premium.

## COMPARING SELF-CONSISTENCY PROMPTING WITH OTHER PROMPTING STRATEGIES

Compared to other prompting strategies, self-consistency prompting generates more accurate results with reasoning-heavy tasks. It's also better at exploring multiple perspectives.

Other strategies, however, are better for other situations. For example, zero-shot is better for simpler and speed-critical tasks, and few-shot is better for mimicking a specific style or tone.

Here's how to consider the different strategies:

- Zero-shot prompting is like asking one person for an answer on the spot.
- One-shot prompting is like showing that person an example before they answer.
- Few-shot prompting is like showing that person multiple examples.
- Role-based prompting is like asking someone to act like a specific person or adopt a specific role and then answer the question like that person or role.
- Chain-of-thought prompting is like asking a person to explain how they got that answer.
- Self-consistency prompting is like asking a question of several people, asking each of them to explain their reasoning and then going with the most common answer.

As you can see, each prompting strategy has its place.

# Summary

In this chapter, you learned about self-consistency prompting—what it is, how it works, and how and when to use it. It's a powerful tool for generating multiple approaches to a given task or problem and then choosing the best approach based on which is most common.

There's more to learn about prompting, however. In the next chapter, you'll learn all about prompt chaining—using multiple prompts to get the output you want.

12

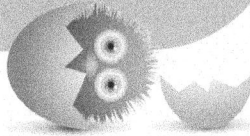

# USING PROMPT CHAINING

Sometimes a single prompt isn't enough. Many tasks require multiple steps to get the desired output, which requires the use of multiple AI prompts—what we call *prompt chaining*. With prompt chaining, multiple prompts are linked together in a sequence, with the output of one prompt used as the input for the next.

# What Prompt Chaining Is and How It Works

Prompt chaining isn't so much a strategy, like few-shot or chain-of-thought prompting, as it is a technique you can use with a variety of prompting strategies. It's a way to work through complex issues in a step-by-step fashion, adjusting your work as you learn more throughout the process.

Prompt chaining involves entering one prompt after another, with subsequent prompts based on the results of the previous prompts. It requires you to break a task down into multiple component parts and then prompt the AI to perform each subtask. The output of one task becomes or informs the input of the next.

The process for using prompt chaining is as follows:

1.  Determine what it is you hope to ultimate accomplish (the end goal).

2.  Break the overall task down into logical subtasks.

3.  Prompt the AI for the initial task.

4.  Use the output from the first task to create or inform the second task.

5.  Repeat step 4 for all additional tasks.

6.  Ask the AI to summarize its results or create an action plan based on the final results.

Prompt chaining works because each new prompt builds on the previous one(s). The AI model remembers your original prompt and all other results created or unearthed along the way. Output is automatically passed between prompts, so there is continuity across multiple steps. It's like the AI is building a house—starting with the foundation and moving up to the roof, building on everything that's been built before.

# Benefits of Prompt Chaining

Prompt chaining offers some unique benefits compared to single-prompt techniques. In particular, prompt chaining provides

- More and better ideas when brainstorming or problem-solving.

- Improved accuracy by moving step-by-step through complex problems.

- The ability to troubleshoot individual steps of a process.

- More control over complex tasks; you decide exactly how each step is handled.

- The ability to use different types of skills and reasoning to attack different components of an issue.

Bottom line, if you have a complex problem, prompt chaining lets you work through an issue step-by-step, adjusting your instructions as you go along.

# When to Use Prompt Chaining

Prompt chaining is a good approach when you're dealing with a large task that won't easily fit within a single prompt, when you have a complex task with multiple steps, or when different steps of a task require different skill sets. Breaking such tasks into multiple tasks makes it easier for the AI to understand what you want and increases accuracy.

The prompt chaining approach is also useful when you're creating content where precision and compliance are critical, such as medical documentation or technical specs. Chaining together multiple prompts lets you review and validate each step before moving on to the next.

In addition, prompt chaining is a good idea when you're working on a task that benefits from feedback and iterative improvement. This lets you build on each previous step, fine-tuning the content or making improvements along the way.

Prompt chaining is also a valid approach when different results require different responses. This type of conditional branching, as you might find in a customer service bot, allows flexible workflows instead of sticking to a single rigid script.

Finally, prompt chaining, like chain-of-thought prompting, helps you maintain a clear audit trail. This is useful for those projects where you need to show each step of the process.

# Examples of Prompt Chaining

It may be easier to understand prompt chaining by looking at some specific examples. It really is as simple as entering the first prompt, examining the results, then using those results to enter a second (and a third and a fourth and on and on) prompt until you get to the final solution.

So here are a few ways you can use prompt chaining in real life.

## Content Creation

One of the more common uses of prompt chaining is to help you create content. That might be an article, blog post, a report, a presentation, a research paper, or even a short story or novel. The content creation process is a complex one that is easily broken down into multiple steps, which makes it ideal for prompt chaining.

In a nutshell, content creation works like this:

1. Brainstorm topics.

2. Choose the desired topic and create an outline.

3. Write a first draft.

4. Edit the draft.

5. Create the final item.

You can work through this process with an AI model using prompt chaining. Start with a brainstorming prompt, like the following:

**Generate 5 ideas for blog posts about pet adoption**

Next, you want to pick the best idea. Use this prompt:

**From this list, pick the most engaging idea and create a detailed outline with four main sections**

Now it's time to start writing. You can approach this on a section-by-section basis, starting with the post's introduction:

**Write an introduction to the post in a conversational tone for a general audience**

Then do the following for each section:

**Write a first draft of the [SECTION] section, building on the content in the previous section.**

Now it's time to refine what was written. In the next prompt, think of the AI as an editor:

**Revise the complete draft for grammar, clarity, and flow.**

That should give you a blog post (or any type of content) that suits your needs.

## Data Analysis

Prompt chaining is particularly useful when you're doing any type of data analysis. When analyzing data, you typically work through the following steps:

1. Gather data.

2. Extract relevant details.

3. Analyze trends.

4. Summarize the results.

Let's look at an example of a competitive analysis of the market for snow blowers. Start with a prompt that gathers the pertinent data:

**List the top five manufacturers of consumer snow blowers for the United States market**

> **NOTE**   Make sure your data request prompt contains the necessary constraints (*consumer* snow blowers and for the *United States* market) to find the precise data you need.

That should give you a list of competitors on which to focus. Now you need to extract from each competitor the information relevant to your analysis. Do so with a prompt like the following:

**For each competitor, find the types of models offered (one-, two-, and three-stage models), battery vs. corded vs. gas powered, clearing width, and price, and present in a table**

The result will be a useful data table with all the key information. Next, you want to have the AI model identify and analyze any trends it finds in the data, focusing on opportunities for your company.

**Based on this table, identify key competitive gaps a new product could fill.**

Now that one or more opportunities have been identified, instruct the AI to write a summary of the results you can present to others in your company.

**Write a one-page executive summary that highlights the biggest opportunities in the market.**

Voilà! Now you're ready to attack the market.

## Problem-Solving

Problem-solving is a multistep process that involves step-by-step reasoning with considerable refinement at each step of the process, the goal being first to brainstorm a number of possible solutions, and then narrow them down to the best option. Depending on the problem, you might follow this sequence of events:

1. Clarify the problem.

2. Generate multiple possible solutions.

3. Evaluate the pros and cons of each option.

4. Narrow it down to the top solutions.

5. Choose a solution.

6. Develop an action plan for the chosen solution.

Start with a prompt that states the problem and helps clarify the issue:

**How can the city reduce traffic accidents in the city center? Clarify the issue and identify key goals and constraints.**

Next, take that output and ask the AI model to generate a set number of potential solutions to the problem.

**Generate 10 possible strategies for addressing this problem and rank them in order of feasibility and effectiveness.**

Next, ask the AI model to evaluate the pros and cons of each offered solution, as follows:

**For each of these strategies, list the key pros and cons in a table.**

Now you have all the information you need to make a decision. The next step, however, is a manual one; you have to choose the solution you want. It may be the first one recommended by the AI model, or you may have a reason for choosing an alternate solution. Whichever solution you choose, the final step is creating an action plan to implement that strategy. Use a prompt like the following:

**Develop a step-by-step plan for implementing the [CHOSEN] solution.**

And there you have it—your problem is solved.

## Decision-Making

Prompt chaining can be used for making any type of decision. You follow the same basic process as in the preceding section, but you fine-tune it for the particular situation.

Let's say, for example, you're trying to decide whether to buy a new automobile or keep your current one for another year. Start by providing the AI model with key details and stating the issue:

**My current car is a 5-year-old Honda Accord with 60,000 miles. It's done what I need it to do with minimal repairs, and I just paid it off. However, my two children are now teenagers and might need more room, plus I'll probably be driving them around more to school and sporting events. I need to decide if I should keep this car for another year or purchase a new model, and if so, what kind? Please identify key factors I should consider when making this decision.**

Okay, that's a lot in one prompt, but most of it is important background information. The AI model should generate a list of things you should consider when making your decision. But don't stop there; next, ask the AI to list the pros and cons of each option.

**List the pros and cons for each option based on these factors and present them in a table.**

We're not done yet. Next, you can ask the AI to assign each factor a score from 1 to 10 and then calculate the total score for each option.

**Assign each factor a score from 1 to 10; then calculate the total for each option.**

The AI will now do what you asked it to do and generate a score for each option. Use this score to help make your decision.

By the way, in this example, if you choose to buy a new car, you then have to decide what type of car to buy. You can also have AI help you with that:

**I'm going to buy a new car. Based on the situation I described, what type of vehicle should I consider?**

You can go even further than that by adding more constraints, asking for specific brand and model recommendations, and the like. AI does all the legwork for you.

## Brainstorming

Finally, you can use prompt chaining to brainstorm ideas on just about any topic. Start by defining the issue, ask for ideas, and then refine the best of them. Here's an example, starting with this prompt:

**Attendance at our city's outdoor youth concerts is declining. Give me 10 reasons why this may be happening.**

That's a good start and tells you what some of the root causes of the problem may be. Now let's get some ideas on how to deal with those problems:

**Give me 10 ideas for dealing with these issues**

That's good, it gets the ball rolling. Now add some constraints:

**We don't have a big promotion budget, and we're limited as to venue and scheduling. Filter out those ideas that aren't feasible given those constraints.**

Now you have a smaller list of more feasible ideas. Let's take the top ones and flesh them out:

**Take the top 3 ideas and provide more details on how to implement them.**

Now, you've progressed from brainstorming a variety of ideas to creating an actionable list and an action plan of the very best options.

# Best Practices for Effective Prompt Chaining

When utilizing the prompt chaining technique, follow these best practices:

- Start with a well-defined end goal.

- Work backward to determine the number of steps needed.

- Don't use too many steps; if you have more than six or eight steps, it can introduce "drift" into the results.

- Keep each step focused on a single specific task; do not group together unrelated actions.

- Include necessary context and details for each step.

- Tell the AI model exactly how to format the output of each step (list, table, and so on)

Finally, make sure to check the results at each stage to ensure that the AI model is staying on track. If you find mistakes in a given step, fix them before moving on to the next step.

# Limitations of Prompt Chaining

Prompt chaining has its limitations. Consider the following:

- Prompt chaining can propagate errors; if any one step produces flawed output, every following step inherits and possibly amplifies that problem.

- Context can be lost over the course of multiple steps; AI can sometimes "forget" details or constraints entered earlier in a lengthy process.

- Similarly, output in later steps can sometimes drift in style or tone from what was produced in previous steps.

Finally, know that prompt chaining is not a simple process. It demands more time and effort than single-prompt techniques, even those with relatively complex prompts. Don't use it if you don't have the time or attention span for it.

# WHEN *NOT* TO USE PROMPT CHAINING

Prompt chaining is useful when you have a longer or more complex task. It's probably best *not* to use prompt chaining in the following instances:

- When you need a quick and simple answer
- When your time is limited
- When your AI resources are limited
- When subsequent prompts in the chain become repetitive
- When earlier prompts yield inaccurate or contradictory results

Put more simply, prompt chaining is best suited for long and complex tasks—and when you have the time and resources to do it. If you have a simpler task that you can explain in a single prompt, there's no need to chain.

# Summary

In this chapter, you learned how to chain prompts together to handle long and/or overly complex tasks. You learned that AI models can pass information from the output of one prompt to the input of another. You also learned how to put together a prompt chain and the best practices for doing so.

In the next chapter, we examine another type of prompt, one that uses a variety of uploaded inputs. It's called multimodal prompting, and it opens up your use of AI to a variety of data formats.

13

# USING MULTIMODAL PROMPTS

AI isn't limited to just text-based prompts. Many AI models let you upload various types of files—text documents, images, videos, and the like—and reference them within a prompt. These additional types of input, called *modes*, let you do things with AI that you can't do with a simple text-based prompt.

# What Is Multimodal Prompting and How Does It Work?

In AI parlance, a type of input is called a *mode*. So, a text-based prompt is one type of mode, and an image file, like a photograph, is another type of mode. A video file is yet another type of mode, as is a Word or Excel document.

When you include two or more different types of input in an AI prompt, it's called *multimodal prompting*. In essence, multimodal prompting is when you give an AI model input in more than one mode.

A multimodal prompt can include any combination of two or more modes. Multimodal prompting includes

- Text prompt plus image file

- Text prompt plus word processing or spreadsheet document

- Text prompt plus audio or video file

- Two or more image files

- Two or more text documents

You get the idea. You can then use one mode to reference or utilize information embedded in another. For example, you could instruct AI to describe, in words, the content of an image. You could also instruct AI to summarize a Word or PDF document, analyze an Excel spreadsheet for trends, or tell you what type of music is included in an audio file.

As to how multimodal prompting works, you first have to upload any files you want to include. Most AI models have an option to upload files, typically a button or link you click and then point to the file you want to upload from your computer.

For example, in ChatGPT, you click the **Add files and more** (plus sign) button in the prompt box and then select either **Add photos & files** or **Add from Google Drive**, as shown in Figure 13.1. The process is similar in Google Gemini, where you click the **Add files** (plus sign) button and then select either **Upload files** or **Add from Drive**, as shown in Figure 13.2. Other AI tools function similarly.

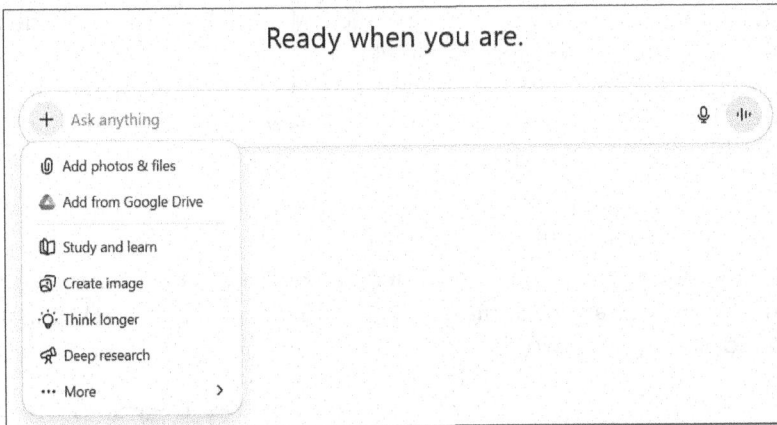

**Ready when you are.**

+ Ask anything

- 📎 Add photos & files
- ☁ Add from Google Drive

- 📖 Study and learn
- 🎨 Create image
- 💡 Think longer
- 🔎 Deep research
- ⋯ More                    >

**FIGURE 13.1**

*Adding a file to a prompt in ChatGPT.*

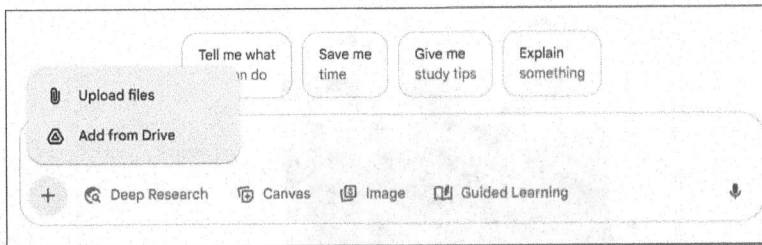

| Tell me what n do | Save me time | Give me study tips | Explain something |

- 📎 Upload files
- ☁ Add from Drive

+   🔍 Deep Research   📋 Canvas   🖼 Image   📖 Guided Learning            🎤

**FIGURE 13.2**

*Adding a file to a prompt in Google Gemini.*

Once you've uploaded the file, you need to tell the AI what to do with it. In most cases, it's a simple matter of referencing the file within a prompt, like this:

**Analyze the spreadsheet I just uploaded and describe any positive or negative trends you find**

or

**Summarize the document I uploaded in a single paragraph**

or

**Explain what the people in the photo are doing**

Multimodal prompting works because the AI model automatically decodes and tries to interpret the content of the files you upload. It combines what it decodes from each input into a single "fusion" layer so that it can analyze and compare them. The AI model then uses learned patterns to produce an output that integrates all the given information.

In addition to accepting inputs in different formats, some AI models can also produce responses in multiple formats. For example, you might ask the AI to **reference the image file within the Word document** or **combine the people in the two photos into a single image**. (Figure 13.3 shows the result of that last prompt: two individuals from two different photos combined into a single image.)

**FIGURE 13.3**

*Two images combined, thanks to Google Gemini.*

# What Kinds of Files Can You Upload?

Most AI tools let you upload the following types of files:

- Text documents from Microsoft Word (.DOCX) or Google Docs, or files in plain text (.TXT) or rich text format (.RTF) files

- Adobe PDF files

- Spreadsheets from Microsoft Excel (.XLSX) or Google Sheets, or files in comma-delimited (.CSV) format

- Presentations from Microsoft PowerPoint (.pptx) or Google Slides

- Images in .PNG, .JPG, .JPEG, .GIF, and .WEBP formats

- Audio files in .MP3 and .WAV formats
- Video files in .MP4 and .MOV formats
- Code in .XLM, HTML, and .JSON formats

Note that not all AI models can handle all of these files types. Some can handle additional formats. When in doubt, just try it.

# When to Use Multimodal Prompting

You should use multimodal prompting when a task involves more than just words. It's the only way to go if the AI needs to see, hear, or otherwise process nontext information alongside a text-based prompt.

> **NOTE**  Images can include photos, drawings, graphs, charts, and diagrams.

It's also the preferred approach when you need to reference, summarize, or analyze text or numbers contained in separate files, such as Word documents, Excel spreadsheets, or PowerPoint presentations. While you *could* enter the information from these files manually, that's a lot of work; it's much easier to upload the file(s) you're working with and let the AI do the data extraction.

# Examples of Multimodal Prompts

There are many different situations where adding one or more files to a traditional AI prompt is either useful or necessary. Table 13.1 presents some examples.

**TABLE 13.1**  Examples of Multimodal Prompts

| Task | Files to Upload | Example Prompt |
|------|-----------------|----------------|
| Describing a photograph or other image | Image file | **Describe what's happening in this photo** |
| Comparing two images | Image files | **Compare these two images and highlight the differences** |
| Brainstorming | Image file | **Using the image as inspiration, generate 5 ideas for marketing slogans that appeal to a 20–30 year old male audience.** |
| Ensuring visual consistency | Image file and text document | **Review the design in the image and determine if it adheres to the brand guidelines in the attached text document. Identify any violations or areas that could be improved.** |

| Task | Files to Upload | Example Prompt |
| --- | --- | --- |
| Comparing text with a data chart or graph | Text document and chart or graph | **Does the chart match the claims in this paragraph?** |
| Analyzing data | Spreadsheet file | **Identify important data trends in this spreadsheet** |
| Summarizing data | Spreadsheet file | **Summarize the key numbers and present in a bulleted list** |
| Comparing data with analysis | Spreadsheet file and text document | **Does the data in the spreadsheet support the claims made in the text document?** |
| Summarizing a meeting recording | Audio file | **Listen to this recording of our weekly meeting and write a one-page bulleted summary** |
| Creating an action list from a meeting recording | Audio file | **Listen to this meeting and create a list of action items** |
| Analyzing music | Audio file | **Listen to this song and tell me what genre it is and who it might appeal to** |
| Describing the contents of a video | Video file | **Describe what is happening in the video. Include descriptions of the main characters and their motivations.** |
| Editing a video | Video file and text document (script) | **Based on this script and footage, suggest appropriate edits to trim 10 minutes from the footage** |
| Fact-checking a video | Video file | **Watch and fact-check the attached video. List all important claims made and whether the claims are accurate.** |
| Turning a video into a presentation | Video file | **Turn the attached video into a 15-minute slide presentation** |
| Extracting insights from a presentation | Presentation file | **Identify the key points in this presentation and output as a bulleted list** |
| Turning a presentation into a report | Presentation file | **Turn the attached presentation into a three-page report, complete with introduction and summary sections** |

There's a lot more you can do with multimodal prompting, of course, but this list should give you some ideas. The key is to be very clear about what you want the AI to do, then give it a shot.

# Best Practices for Multimodal Prompting

When you're uploading files for multimodal prompting, keep these best practices in mind:

- State your goal clearly; make sure you tell the AI exactly what you want it to do with each type of input.

- Clearly reference the input file(s); this is particularly important when you've uploaded more than one file.

- Ask focused questions; instead of saying "tell me what you see," ask the AI to "identify the three relevant properties in the painting."

- Break down any multistep reasoning; ask the AI to handle each modality separate from the others.

- Consider giving context for accuracy; for example, note whether this is for a financial analysis, medical evaluation, or child's notebook.

You'll also need to keep file size into account. Some AI tools may have limits on file size, which means you may need to resize larger files. Just make sure that image files have a high-enough resolution to be easily readable.

# Limitations of Multimodal Prompting

Multimodal prompting can be challenging to get right. You may want an AI model to perform certain file-related tasks that it simply can't do. When crafting a multimodal prompt, keep these limitations in mind:

- Some AI models may have limitations on file size.

- Not all AI models are compatible with all file formats.

- Low-resolution, blurry, or otherwise poor-quality images may be difficult to analyze.

- AI models may have difficulty extracting text from images or PDF files, resulting in incorrect characters or formatting.

- Descriptions of images, videos, and audio can be subjective; the AI may look at things different than you do.

- Multimodal analysis of large images and video files can consume more processing resources and take more time to complete.

Multimodal prompting is one of the newer and more complex types of AI tasking, so be prepared for some hiccups along the way. If you don't like the results from one AI model, try another one and see what happens.

# Summary

In this chapter, you learned how to utilize different types of files in multimodal prompts. You learned when and how to use multimodal prompting, as well as the various limitations of the technique.

In the next chapter, you'll learn how to evaluate the prompts you create.

# 14

# EVALUATING PROMPT PERFORMANCE

You now know how to construct all manner of AI prompts. But how do you know if your prompting strategy is effective?

If you're serious about improving your AI prompting, you need some way to evaluate prompt performance. Fortunately, there are several ways you can determine whether your prompts are working as well as they should, and this chapter covers all of them.

# Why Prompt Evaluation Matters

Evaluating the performance of your prompts ensures that you're getting the best possible results—and the fewest possible errors. This is especially important if you do a lot of prompting or if your prompting involves mission-critical tasks.

Prompt evaluation goes beyond testing whether the answer provided was right or wrong. (Although accuracy is extremely important, without question.) Prompt evaluation involves determining the relevancy of results (in terms of content, level, and tone/style), prompt generation speed, the safety of the results, and, of course, the accuracy of results.

It's important that the results you receive

- Answer the question or perform the task you provided

- Are error-free

- Are based on up-to-date data

- Are appropriate for your intended audience

- Meet all other requirements posed or implied in the prompt

A given response might be technically accurate but not complete. It may be accurate but presented in an inappropriate fashion. It may be accurate but pitched at the wrong interest level. It may be accurate but not formatted correctly.

Prompt evaluation can tell you how well any given AI model is doing with the prompts you present. Any less-than-perfect results may be the fault of the AI, or it may be because your prompts could use improvement.

Evaluating your prompts can have noticeable benefits, including

- Improved accuracy

- Results that are more optimized for specific goals

- Enhanced user experience

- More efficient use of AI resources (which could result in lower processing costs)

In short, when you practice prompt evaluation, you get better results. That's a good thing.

# Defining Prompt Performance Metrics

How, exactly, do you determine whether a prompt was successful? To do so, you first need to define a set of metrics that measure prompt performance. These metrics can be both quantitative and qualitative.

## Quantitative Metrics

One way to evaluate the effectiveness of a prompt is to use quantitative metrics—things you can objectively measure, typically numerically. There are several different quantitative metrics to consider.

First, and perhaps most important, is the response's accuracy. The AI output must be factually correct as well as respond to any parameters or constraints included in the prompt. If a response doesn't deliver what you asked, in a full and correct manner, it has failed.

Accuracy isn't the only quantitative metric you can use to evaluate prompt performance, however. Consider the following measurable metrics you can employ:

- **Success rate:** What percentage of queries produced usable responses without requiring human intervention or rerunning the prompt?

- **Consistency:** Does the AI generate the same or similar results over repeated runs? You can score this by calculating the percentage of responses that exactly match the expected output. Also, be sure to consider semantic accuracy, where the responses are correct even if the wording of the responses differs.

- **Response time:** How long did it take for the AI to generate its output?

- **Output length:** How long is the response? (Know, however, that the quantity of the output does not necessarily reflect the quality of said output.)

- **Constraint satisfaction:** What percentage of responses followed the specific formatting rules, length requirements, or other constraints?

- **Resource usage:** For those models that employ usage tokens, how many tokens were used per input and output, and in total?

## Qualitative Metrics

Most measurements of prompt performance are more subjective. That is, they're based on observation and judgment rather than on anything you can numerically quantify.

Some of the more important qualitative metrics include

- **Relevance:** How well does the response address the question or task?

- **Completeness:** Does the response cover all necessary aspects of the query? Are there any gaps in the response that require follow-up prompting?

- **Coherence and flow:** Is the response logically organized and easy to follow? Does it have a clear structure and smooth transitions?

- **Clarity:** Is the response easy to understand by the target audience? Does it employ the appropriate vocabulary, sentence structure, and depth of content?

- **Conciseness:** Is the response thorough without being unnecessarily verbose?

- **Tone and voice:** Does the response match the desired communication style for the specified audience?

- **Formatting:** Does the response follow any specified formatting constraints?

- **Engagement:** How compelling, interesting, or motivating is the response? Does it appropriately inform, persuade, or entertain the intended audience?

- **Appropriateness:** Is the response suitable for the context, audience, and intended use case? Is it culturally sensitive, and does it meet professional standards?

- **Actionable:** For instructional or advisory tasks, how practical and implementable is the output?

- **Empathy and understanding:** Does the response demonstrate an appropriate understanding of human emotions, concerns, and perspectives?

- **Bias and harm:** Does the output exhibit any unfair treatment of stereotyping of specific groups? Is the content harmful in any way?

- **Trustworthiness:** Does the response feel reliable and authoritative? Does it instill confidence for the intended audience?

- **Creativity:** For creative tasks, how imaginative, unique, or innovative is the response?

- **User experience:** What is the overall user satisfaction with the AI for this task?

## USING MULTIPLE METRICS

In many instances, effective prompt evaluation requires a combination of multiple metrics relevant to the task at hand. For example, if you're evaluating a customer service chatbot, you might track accuracy, response time, constraint satisfaction, and customer satisfaction. In contrast, evaluating a content generation system might require tracking creativity, coherence, and formatting compliance.

The point is to employ those metrics that best evaluate what it is you're trying to accomplish. Don't use metrics that have little or no relevance to the task, just because you can. The effectiveness of a prompt must be judged in accordance with the intended task.

# Simple Ways to Evaluate Prompt Performance

Given the various metrics you can use to measure prompt performance, how do you go about evaluating that performance? The simplest approaches focus on qualitative metrics and involve observing and evaluating AI's response to a given prompt or series of prompts.

## Manual Review

The first approach is a basic manual review—what some call a "human-in-the-loop" approach. This is the most straightforward method, where you simply look at the AI's output to a given prompt and decide, qualitatively, whether it's acceptable. You can use any or all of the qualitative metrics I just covered, but you have to be the judge of whether the prompt satisfies these basic requirements. (Is it accurate? Is it understandable? Is it formatted correctly?)

With this type of manual review, it helps to develop a simple rating scale to determine prompt effectiveness. You can go with a simple yes/no approach or rate the response on a scale of 1 to 5 for each of the applicable metrics. Enter your results in a spreadsheet so you can compare different prompts and variations.

## A/B Testing

The second approach is the side-by-side comparison. This type of A/B testing lets you try two different versions of a prompt, changing a single parameter each time, to see which performs best.

Run the first prompt and then run the second; then evaluate both and compare the results. This helps you quickly identify which prompt parameters are more effective for your specific task.

> **NOTE**   When doing A/B testing, change only one element in a prompt at a time. For example, you might do one prompt with a specified role and one without, change the tone for one of the prompts, or add a constraint to one of them. This lets you determine which individual parameters make the most difference in the AI performance.

## Using AI to Evaluate Itself

This is an interesting approach to prompt evaluation, letting an AI model evaluate its own responses. It essentially takes a lot of the work out of an otherwise manual review.

To use this approach, start by running the prompt you want to evaluate. Next, copy the original prompt and the AI response back into the AI model, and instruct it as follows:

**Rate this response on a scale of 1 to 5 for [PARAMETERS]**

Replace [PARAMETERS] with the specific parameters you want evaluated. For example, you might want to evaluate the accuracy and clarity of a given response, so you'd enter the prompt:

**Rate this response on a scale of 1 to 5 for accuracy and clarity**

Note that you can also use a different AI model to evaluate the response from the original model. For example, you might run the original prompt in ChatGPT, then copy the prompt and response into Google Gemini for evaluation.

# Advanced Prompt Evaluation

For most casual users, the simple prompt evaluation methods I just discussed are more than adequate. Professional users, however, might want to use more advanced methods to evaluate the effectiveness of their prompts.

I don't go into too much detail on these advanced methods because they really are for more advanced or professional users, but some of the more popular approaches include

- **Expert review:** Use subject-matter experts to evaluate the accuracy and appropriateness of a response.

- **Rule-based validation:** Compare the AI results to a predefined set of objective rules or criteria.

- **Similarity scoring:** Converts a text response into numerical representations and then calculates the mathematical distance between the response and a reference answer. There are several different ways to employ this method, including cosine similarity, Bilingual Evaluation Understudy (BLEU), and Recall-Oriented Understudy for Gisting Evaluation (ROUGE), each of which is best tailored for specific types of tasks.

- **F1 scoring:** This numeric approach evaluates a response's trade-off between precision (accuracy) and recall (completeness).

- **BERTScoring:** An advanced metric that uses a pre-trained language model to understand the semantic meaning of words in a response to determine how well the response matches a reference text.

- **Perplexity:** A way to measure how surprised or "perplexed" an AI model is when it encounters new text. In essence, it assesses how well a model can predict a sample of text.

As you can see, these advanced evaluation methods are not for amateurs. They can precisely and quantitatively measure the performance of any given AI prompt and are best employed in professional settings.

# Best Practices for Prompt Evaluation

Whichever approach you use to evaluate the performance of your AI prompts, keep these best practices in mind:

- Before you start evaluating, define one or more specific and measurable objectives.

- Use your current performance to establish a baseline to determine if suggested improvements are meaningful.

- Be specific in your prompts; vague prompts are difficult to meaningfully evaluate.

- Focus on one parameter at a time; if you change up too many things between prompts, you won't know which change had the biggest effect.

- Track your results, even if it's just in a simple spreadsheet or word processing document.

- Iterate and improve; use evaluation results to refine your prompts over multiple runs.

# Common Pitfalls When Evaluating Prompt Performance

You should also be aware of several pitfalls that can affect your prompt evaluation.

First, know that AI results can include bias or harmful content. You may need to manually identify such content and adjust the evaluation accordingly.

Similarly, you need to be aware of any bias in your human evaluators. (That includes any personal bias if you're doing the evaluating.) Remember that subjective evaluations are just that—subjective.

Next, know that some variability in outputs is entirely random. You'll need to conduct multiple tests to smooth out the randomness and identify the real trends.

You should also avoid *overfitting* your evaluation for specific test cases. That is, there's a risk of focusing too much on the details of past prompts so that you're unable to generalize your findings to future prompts. Not that details aren't important, but you need to be able to generalize what you've learned when conditions change.

In addition, don't fall into the trap of confusing output length with quality. Just because a response uses more words doesn't mean it's better. Quite often, the more concise output is the better response.

Finally, remember the context. What constitutes an acceptable response is highly dependent on the user's intent and how the application will be used.

# Summary

In this chapter, you learned why evaluating prompt performance is important. You also learned several different ways to evaluate performance, including key metrics to consider. Prompt evaluation is part art and part science, and it takes some time and experience to master.

In the next chapter, you'll learn how to use your prompt evaluations to refine and reframe your prompts for better results.

# 15

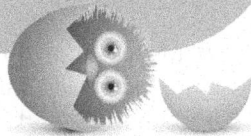

# REFINING YOUR PROMPTS

If you want to get better at AI prompting, you have to learn how to refine your prompts. That means reworking your prompts in successive runs to achieve better or different results. That's typically done by reframing or rewording your prompts, in what we call iterative or reflective prompting.

# Why It's Important to Refine Your Prompts

Why is it important to learn how to refine your prompts? It's simple: The first drafts of your prompts are rarely perfect. Yeah, sometimes you'll hit it out of the ballpark on your first swing, but more often than not, your first prompt will only get you close to what you want. To achieve better results, you have to refine your prompts in an iterative process.

Iterative prompting is the process of refining a prompt over multiple runs. You start out with the first draft of your prompt, evaluate the results, make a few changes to the prompt, and run it again. You repeat this process until you get the desired results.

If you *don't* engage in iterative prompting, you're stuck with the first result generated. That may be good enough, especially if the task or question is a simple one. But for more complex tasks, you need to work with the AI model until it "gets" exactly what you're asking for. You fine-tune the prompt each time through, essentially learning from the results of each run.

When I use the word *learning*, it's important to know that both you and the AI model are learning. You're learning from any inaccuracies or missteps in the results how to tweak the prompt to get the AI more on track. The AI, in turn, learns from each run to deliver results that are more like what you're asking for. It's a matter of reflecting on each subsequent run to make the next run even better.

# How Iterative Prompting Works

The iterative prompting process consists of four steps in a continuing feedback loop, as shown in Figure 15.1.

1. **Prompt:** You create and run the first prompt.

2. **Response:** AI delivers the response.

3. **Reflect:** You reflect on the accuracy and quality of the output.

4. **Revise:** You revise the initial prompt and return to step 1.

After you revise the prompt, you start the process all over again by running the revised prompt. The process continues in a loop until you're satisfied with the results.

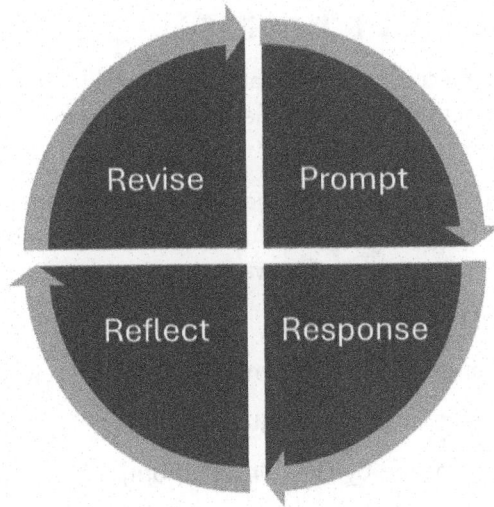

**FIGURE 15.1**

*The iterative prompting process.*

The reflection step may be the most important here. You need to evaluate the initial AI response and reflect on the accuracy and appropriateness of that response. Ask questions, such as these:

- Was the response accurate?

- Was the response complete?

- Was the response clear and understandable?

- Was the response overly broad or vague?

- Was the response formatted as requested?

- Was the response presented at the requested level or to the requested audience?

- Did the response contain any irrelevant or inappropriate information?

- Was the response exactly what you wanted? If not, what would you want to change?

In essence, you want to examine the strengths and weaknesses of the response and use that information to make any necessary changes to the prompt.

# How to Refine Your Prompts

After you've reflected on and evaluated the initial response, you're a little smarter about how to direct the AI to get the results you want. Use those smarts to refine the prompt to run again.

How can you refine a prompt? It's not about starting from scratch and rewriting the entire thing. No, it's about making minor changes—*refinements*—that can better direct the AI to the results you want.

What types of refinements can you make? Consider the following:

- Reword the prompt to better emphasize the main focus
- Clarify the intent by adding context or details
- Reframe the question by changing the format or perspective
- Add or remove constraints, such as word limits, tone, formatting, and the like
- If the AI appears confused by a big or complex task, break it into multiple smaller tasks chained together

In short, determine what the AI got wrong (or could improve) and then edit the part of the prompt that led to the issue. An AI model either can't or won't tell you that it's confused; you have to figure that out and refine your prompt to eliminate the confusion.

# Best Practices for Iterative Prompting

When reworking your prompts in subsequent runs, follow these best practices:

- Make your initial prompt simple; then add details as you refine it in subsequent runs.
- After each run, ask yourself if it got you closer to your goal.
- On subsequent runs, determine what's still missing.
- Start by making small tweaks, not major rewrites.
- Change just one variable at a time.

> **NOTE** If you're not sure what you should change on the next run, you can ask the AI model: **suggest improvements to this prompt.**

# Pitfalls When Iterative Prompting

When revising your prompts, there are a few potential pitfalls to ponder.

First, beware of changing too many variables between prompts. If you change more than one thing and the results improve, you don't know *which* thing you changed led to the improvement. Iterate systematically.

Second, don't revise a prompt just to revise a prompt. Make sure you have a clear goal in mind and make changes to move closer to that goal.

Next, know that the more prompts you run, the further away you may get from your original intent. This is called *context drift*, and it happens when the AI model "forgets" some of the original instructions or context. You can prevent this by periodically summarizing and restating the most important context and constraints.

In addition, any bias present in a prompt or that creeps into a response will get reinforced in subsequent runs. It's kind of an echo chamber effect and can also reinforce particular viewpoints at the exclusion of others. Be aware of your own assumptions and biases during the entire process.

Finally, iterative prompting is a slow and tedious process. You have to take the time to evaluate the response from each run, determine what changes to make, and then run the prompt again—multiple times. If you don't have the time or the patience to do this, you won't like the process.

# Summary

In this chapter, you learned how to use iterative prompting to improve prompt results over multiple runs. You learned how to refine your prompts and how to avoid common pitfalls.

Next, we look at how to create prompts for specific tasks. First up: prompts for different types of writing!

16

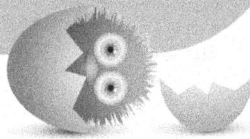

# PROMPTING FOR WRITING

One of the most popular uses of AI is for writing—any type of writing. You can use AI to write social media posts, text messages, and emails. You can use AI to write reports for school or work. You can use AI to write instruction manuals and product specifications. You can even use AI to write children's stories, poetry, and novels.

When you're using AI to help with your writing, any type of writing, the key to success is all in the prompt. The more specific the prompt you create, the more you'll like what AI writes for you.

# Why Use AI for Writing

While some professional writers use artificial intelligence to augment their writing, AI is more often used as a tool by nonwriters who need to write something but aren't quite sure how. AI can help any regular person appear as if they're a skilled writer, even if they have trouble putting two sentences together on their own.

In this regard, AI can be a lifesaver. Whether you need to write a letter to a distant relative, a Facebook post about an upcoming event, or a paper for school or work, AI can help you do it—or just do it for you. AI can help you get started, come up with interesting ideas, and turn those ideas into words. All you need to do is create the appropriate prompt.

Consider just some of the reasons that regular people and professional writers alike turn to AI for assistance:

- Overcoming writer's block; let AI get the ball started for you
- Generating creative ideas
- Expanding rough ideas into finished pieces
- Creating outlines that provide structure and organization for longer works
- Doing the research necessary for many types of writing
- Creating first drafts of works that you later finish
- Assisting with tasks that require a lot of content quickly, such as blog posts, social media captions, and the like
- Checking and correcting grammar, spelling, and punctuation
- Editing a piece for conciseness, tone, and style
- Paraphrasing brief passages
- Rewriting entire pieces
- Optimizing content for search engines (search engine optimization)
- Speeding up the writing process (AI can often put words on "paper" faster than you can.)

In addition, many businesses find that using AI-created content helps them reduce costs. Instead of paying professional writers, they can generate their own content at low or no cost using AI writing tools.

**NOTE**  As a professional writer who has often been "replaced" when businesses shift to AI-generated content, I find this trend disturbing. I always recommend that businesses that want to get the best possible results use professional writers instead of AI. The human touch ensures that professionally written content stands out from the average AI-generated content.

## TYPES OF THINGS AI CAN HELP YOU WRITE

AI can help you write all sorts of things. This is especially helpful if you don't consider yourself a strong writer or if you actually hate writing. Whatever it is you need to write, AI can help you do it.

This includes:

- Advertising and marketing copy
- Articles (print and online)
- Biographies
- Blog posts
- Children's stories
- Contracts and other legal documents
- E-books
- Emails
- How-to instructions
- Letters
- Newsletters
- Novels
- Poems
- Presentations
- Product descriptions
- Proposals
- Research reports
- School papers
- Scripts
- Short stories
- Social media posts
- Technical specifications
- Text messages
- User manuals and guides

And, of course, a lot more. Just about anything you need to write, AI can help you write it.

# Discovering the Best AI Tools for Writing

Writing is one of the many things that most general AI tools do well. That means you can easily use tools such as ChatGPT, DeepSeek, and Google Gemini to do your writing for you.

There are also a handful of AI tools that are fine-tuned specifically for various types of writing tasks. These include

- Jasper (www.jasper.ai), designed specifically for marketers and marketing-related projects

- Paperpal (https://paperpal.com), designed for academic writing

- Rytr (https://rytr.me), for all types of short-form content

- Sudowrite (https://sudowrite.com), designed primarily for fiction writing

These task-specific AI writing tools might be worth checking out, especially if they meet your specific writing needs.

> **NOTE**   Most people eschew these dedicated AI writing tools and instead use ChatGPT, Google Gemini, and other general AI tools for their writing needs.

# Key Prompt Parameters for Writing

As with all types of AI prompts, constructing a prompt for a written project is as simple and as complex as instructing the AI model to create exactly what you want. The key is to provide a clear, detailed, and inclusive set of instructions that help the AI create a specific type of content.

To best instruct any AI tool, your prompt should include all necessary parameters that describe your project. Table 16.1 provides a list of the most typical parameters for all types of written projects.

**TABLE 16.1**   Parameters for Writing-Related Prompts

| Parameter | Description |
| --- | --- |
| Task | What you want the AI to write, such an essay, a report, an article, and so forth |
| Topic/theme | What the work is about; be as specific as possible |
| Style or tone | The "voice" of the project, such as formal, informal, humorous, academic, conversational, and so forth |
| Structure | Specific sections that need to be included, listed in order, such as introduction, body, and summary |
| Headings | Along with the structure, specify any desired headings and subheadings to include |
| Length | In characters, words, or pages, the minimum and/or maximum length of the project |

| Parameter | Description |
|---|---|
| Audience | Who will be reading the work |
| Reading level | The target reading level for the finished work, typically by grade level |
| Key concepts | Key concepts or ideas that should be included in the project |
| Perspective | Presented if the project should present a specific argument or perspective |
| Characters | For works of fiction, names, descriptions, and characteristics of key characters |
| Plot | For works of fiction |
| Role/persona | Include when you want the AI to assume a specific persona or point of view, such as a high school English teacher, a professional copywriter, or a news commentator |
| Output format | What you want the completed project to look like, such as **a promotional email, a bulleted list**, or **an academic report in MLA format** |
| Research requirements | For research papers or reports, any research requirements; include any resources that should be used |
| Context | Include any necessary background information that might help the AI complete the task |
| Constraints | Instruct the AI what *not* to do, such as **avoid using jargon** or **don't include any explicit opinions** |

When you appropriately use the appropriate parameters, you should get a response that comes at least somewhat close to what you wanted. The more parameters you include, and the more specific you describe each parameter, the better the output will be.

# Examples of Prompts for Different Types of Writing

How do you combine these parameters into an effective AI prompt? Here are some examples:

**Write a one-page letter to my Aunt Lorainne thanking her for the sweater she gave me for Christmas and inviting her to our house for the Thanksgiving holiday.**

**Write a 500-word blog post ranking the 10 best albums of the 1980s. I'm a particular fan of the early MTV era, Prince, Elvis Costello, and the Police.**

**Write a short Facebook post telling my friends about my new car, a gray SUV with three-row seating for all my kids and their friends.**

Write an email to my son's third-grade teacher, gently complaining about the amount of homework she's assigning and how Heather has trouble getting through it all each night.

Write an editorial for my local newspaper complaining about a proposed low-income development project. Avoid any racial bias but emphasize how such a project can lower property values.

As the president of the neighborhood association, write an email to all neighbors announcing the change in trash pickup from Tuesdays to Wednesdays. Remind them that cans need to be out by 7 am that day but shouldn't be left out overnight.

Write a script for a 15-minute podcast about Medicare for seniors. Focus on the different types of plans available and the pros and cons of traditional Medicare vs. Medicare Advantage plans. No guests, just me talking. Separate different segments with short music clips. Suggest some appropriate music for these clips. The podcast is for tech-savvy seniors.

Write a short story about a teenaged girl named Claire who discovers a hidden world within her reflection in the mirror. The audience is young adult readers.

Write a 2000-word article for a general music site about the career of Paul McCartney. Including sections on Life Before the Beatles, The Fab Four, Wings, and Solo Works. Make sure it's written at an 8th grade level.

Write a 16-line poem about the changing seasons. Include a variety of sensory details to describe the sights, sounds, and smells of each season.

Write a 1000-word essay that argues against the use of standardized testing in schools. Include arguments that address the inherent racial and gender biases in standardized testing.

Write a two-page analysis of the book Slaughterhouse-Five for a high school English class. Explore major themes, characters, and literary devices. Discuss how the author's background informed the plotline and details in the book. Include at least three citations in MLA format.

Assume that you are a movie critic and write a comparative analysis of the original movie version of West Side Story and Steven Spielberg's recent remake. Explore the similarities and differences in style, execution, and underlying themes. The article should be written for possible publication in a major academic journal.

Write an entry for my personal journal about my child's first day of kindergarten. Her name is Jamie and she was very excited to meet her teacher and make new friends, but very nervous about being left at school without me. I had to stick around for a half hour for her to get accustomed to the new environment, but then she did fine.

Write a 2000-word travelogue for travelers about vacationing in San Diego. Focus on family-friendly things to do, places to eat, and places to stay. Be mildly but not overtly promotional about San Diego tourism.

Write a comprehensive instruction manual for replacing a kitchen faucet. Make sure the instructions include optional soap dispenser and filtered water. Recommend additional resources at the end.

I'm writing a college textbook titled The Modern Presidency. I need help with the chapter on President Eisenhower. Can you write a first draft of this chapter, about 20 pages long, for a student audience? Include questions at the end of the chapter.

Write a 1000-word report on the effect of plastic bottles on the environment. This is for a middle-school science class and needs to be in MLA format with at least three citations.

Write a promotional email announcing a new product for musicians called The Magic Ear, which is a new type of in-ear monitor with superior noise reduction. The product is priced at $299 but available for a limited time only for just $199. Perfect for any musician on stage.

Write a haiku about the sound of crickets

# Best Practices for Writing with AI

When crafting a prompt for a written project, keep these best practices in mind:

- Precisely describe the project, the required style and tone, and the audience, along with other key parameters.

- Use action words, such as *write*, *summarize*, and *explain* to tell the AI what to do.

- For more complex prompts, separate sections with a separator, such as dashes or hash marks; you can also use headings within the prompt.

- For less common or more complex types of projects, include an example of similar output.

- If you don't like the first result, rerun the prompt either as-is or with refined parameters; you also might want to try running the prompt with a different AI tool to see what you get.

Again, the key for using AI for writing is to define in the prompt the desired output in as much detail as possible. Don't just say, **write a short story about pirates**; instead, say, **write a 1000-word short story for an elementary school audience about funny pirates encountering a mischievous whale**. The more details, the better.

> **NOTE**  As useful as AI is for writing, better results often come from combining AI with human skills. Let AI help with the outline and initial drafts, and maybe even the final editing, but do the actual writing yourself. If you let AI take over the entire writing process, you're not writing—you're just prompting.

## USING AI FOR INSPIRATION AND OUTLINING

AI isn't just for writing a finished piece. You can also use AI to generate ideas and help to put your ideas in order.

When you're facing a blank page, ask AI to generate a set number of ideas, whether they be for the plot of a piece of fiction or the contents of a report. Use a prompt like this one:

**Generate five ideas for an article about organic gardening to pitch to my local newspaper**

You can then take the best of those ideas to expand into a full piece. (Or you can have AI do the writing.)

In terms of organizing your ideas, AI is great for creating outlines. Use a prompt like the following:

**Create an outline for a 2000-word literary paper discussing the evolution of film noir in modern cinema.**

You can add any specific topics you want included, then let the AI do its thing. Writing the finished piece is then as easy as filling in the blanks.

## Summary

In this chapter, you learned how to create AI prompts for various types of writing, including the most common and useful parameters to use in your prompts. AI is getting pretty good at the writing thing; you just have to make sure you do a good job describing what you want it to write, and for what audience.

Next, we move into the business world and learn how to craft the best AI prompts for various types of productivity-related tasks.

17

# PROMPTING FOR PRODUCTIVITY

AI is being adopted by organizations both big and small to help improve their productivity. AI can do many things faster and more accurately than humans can; it can also assist human workers by doing a lot of the grunt work involved with almost any task.

The key, as with any use of AI, is properly prompting the AI tool about the work that needs to be done. Productivity prompting can help increase your personal productivity, but only when done correctly.

# Three Principles of Productivity Prompting

When using AI for productivity, whether that's in business, education, or your personal life, it's important to correctly set your expectations. While AI can automate some of your work, it can't do the entire job. You need to think of AI as a highly capable junior assistant, helping you get your work done—as long as you provide the AI with the same instructions and support you'd give a human assistant.

With that in mind, there are three core principles involved when prompting for productivity:

- Clarity
- Context
- Constraints

The next sections examine each in more detail.

## Clarity

When writing prompts for productivity-related tasks, you need to be specific, concise, and goal-oriented. Tell the AI precisely what you want it to do, in as much detail as possible. Don't leave much—if anything—open to the AI's interpretation.

It's important to remember that using AI for productivity is more than just asking questions. Instead, you're designing a process for the AI to follow and delegating tasks to the AI. The more clarity you provide, the better the AI can do what is asked of it.

## Context

It's also important that you provide the AI with all the information it needs to complete the task at hand. That means providing the necessary background information so that the AI understands your intent.

That background information can and, in most cases, should include the following:

- **Audience:** Who this project is for (upper management, colleagues, customers, and so forth)
- **Tone:** The approach, word choice, and formality of the output (professional, enthusiastic, motivational, and so forth)
- **Format:** How the output should be presented and structured (bullet points, tables, and so on)
- **Length:** In words, pages, and numbers of slides in a presentation

For some tasks, you can provide this background information in the form of a reference document. With this approach, you essentially show the AI what you want the output to look like.

> **NOTE**  Learn more about using reference documents in Chapter 7, "Using One-Shot Prompting."

## Constraints

The final principle of productivity prompting involves constraints—telling AI what *not* to do or include. Constraints are those boundaries that help the AI stay on track and avoid meandering or irrelevant results.

Constraints can involve content, tone, format, length, and other parameters. If you're asking AI to analyze pricing trends, for example, you might tell it not to include closeout merchandise in the analysis. Or if you want AI to propose some brainstorming ideas, you might tell it to avoid ideas that are too costly or outside the scope of a project.

By using constraints, you narrow the AI's possible suggestions to those that are actually useful to you. This helps breed creativity while providing a necessary focus.

# Common Productivity Uses of AI

AI can assist practically all aspects of a business, as well as the productivity tasks you undertake in your personal life. We can't cover all possible productivity use cases here, but this section looks at some of the most common uses of AI as a productivity tool.

## Writing and Communication

AI can assist with all types of business and professional writing—drafting emails and memos, writing reports, creating speeches and presentations, you name it. AI excels at translating complex ideas into simple explanations, whatever the medium may be.

> **NOTE**  Chapter 16, "Prompting for Writing," covers more about AI-generated writing.

When crafting a prompt for any type of communication, include the following elements:

- Task (what you want AI to do)
- Topic/theme

- Style/tone

- Structure

- Length

- Audience

- Output format

For example, if you want to create a one-page memo advising a company's staff to submit their expense reports by a certain day of the month, you might craft the following prompt:

**Write a one-page memo to all company employees. The topic should be "Expense Reports," and the memo should be straightforward and professional. The memo should advise staff that all expense reports for a given month should be submitted by the 10th of the following month and use the standard company forms. All expense reports should be submitted to one's direct superior and include all necessary documentation, such as receipts. Any questions should be directed to the HR department. Create the memo in Word format.**

If you need to give a speech at a business luncheon about how small businesses can use artificial intelligence, you might create the following prompt:

**Draft a 15-minute speech for the association of local small businesses. The speech should be about how small businesses can use AI to streamline their operations and better reach their customers. Use casual language and don't expect the audience to know much about AI or care about the technical details of how it works. The tone should be personable but still professional, like one businessperson to another.**

You can also use AI to create slides for presentations. You might use a prompt like the following:

**Create a PowerPoint presentation, no more than 20 slides, to convince my homeowner's association to create a neighborhood watch. Be persuasive and include relevant statistics. Make the presentation more visual than text-based and use bullet points instead of text paragraphs. The presentation should be persuasive and include a call to action.**

Another good use of AI is to summarize longer documents. If you want AI to summarize a long report in a series of bullet points for easier consumption, consider the following prompt (accompanying your upload of the original document):

**Summarize the attached document in a single page, using easy-to-understand bullet points. The audience is upper management who don't have the time to read the complete report. Include a section for action items.**

As you can see, all these tasks are facilitated when you include the proper instructions about content, tone, audience, and output.

# Marketing and Promotion

Marketing professionals can use AI to brainstorm concepts, generate ideas, create action plans, and execute those plans. In this fashion, AI can enhance the creative process and speed up some of the drudge work associated with creating marketing materials.

When using AI in a marketing capacity, include the following information in your prompts:

- Task (what you want AI to do)
- Topic
- Context (background info)
- Role (the persona AI should assume)
- Audience
- Output format

For example, if you want AI to generate some ideas for an upcoming marketing campaign, you might use the following prompt:

**Generate 5 ideas for a campaign to market the company's new six-blade razor. Consider similar products from competitors and any competitive advantages our product might have. The target customer is middle-aged men with moderate-to-high incomes.**

Perhaps you want AI to write the copy for an online ad for that product. Consider the following prompt:

**Write copy for an online advertisement for our six-blade razor. Target audience is middle-aged men with moderate-to-high incomes. Copy should mention performance and results and be no more than four sentences long. Include a catchy title.**

AI can also help you create detailed marketing plans. Use a prompt similar to the following:

**Create a strategic marketing plan to introduce our new six-blade razor. We want to achieve a market share of 20% within the first year of release. Include pricing, distribution, and media.**

AI won't replace experienced marketers, but it will help them be more effective and more efficient.

## Planning and Organization

AI has proven useful for managing time and projects. You can use AI to create meeting agendas, project timelines, task breakdowns, and similar tasks.

When using AI for planning and organization, use the following parameters in your prompts:

- Task (what you want AI to do)
- Topic
- Goal
- Key milestones and priorities
- Dependencies
- Availability and time blocking
- Audience
- Output format

For example, if you want to create a project plan for the launch of a new initiative, you might use the following prompt:

**Generate a project plan to launch the organization's new website. We want the site to go live in 4 weeks. Include key milestones, tasks, and potential dependencies.**

You can also use AI to optimize your daily schedule. You'll need to provide your current schedule by uploading a calendar file or meeting list; then create a prompt like this one:

**Analyze my calendar and to-do list in the attached files and create a time-blocked daily schedule for my work week. Allow at least 4 hours a day, in contiguous 2-hour minimum blocks, for me to work independently. Prioritize client meetings and meetings with upper management. Deprioritize perfunctory meetings with other departments.**

Here's another popular use of AI: summarizing meetings and creating meeting notes. If you have an audio recording of a meeting, you can upload that file to the AI and then ask it to summarize the meeting, like this:

**Listen to the attached audio file of our monthly management meeting. Please provide a one-page summary of the meeting, along with a bullet-point to-do list organized by department, to distribute to the management team.**

## Education and Learning

AI is already being widely used in education—and not just for students looking for a little behind-the-scenes help. Educators can use AI to create lesson plans and personalized training, as well as create content for use in class and generate and grade student tests.

When creating prompts for these tasks, educators should consider the following parameters:

- Task (what you want AI to do)
- Topic (both general and specific)
- Grade level
- Level of difficulty
- Output format

For example, you might use AI to prepare for the next day's classwork on a given topic and craft a prompt like the following:

**You are a 10th grade physics teacher. Tomorrow's class will discuss quantum entanglement. Provide a detailed guide for how to present this topic to the class, who are currently working at an advanced level. Provide one explanation using a simple analogy, another using a bullet-point summary of key principles, and another that uses the example of a real-world experiment that proved the theory.**

Or, perhaps, you want to create a lesson plan for the entire semester. Create a prompt like this one:

**Assume you are a 8th grade music teacher. Create a lesson plan for the semester that includes an overview of European classical music as well as 20th and 21st century popular music. Also include sections on basic music theory, including tones, note values, and scales. The music class meets two days a week. Provide additional material for the more advanced students or those already taking music lessons on an instrument.**

Within a class, you can use AI to create worksheets, study guides, and the like. You can use prompts like the following:

**Create a math worksheet for 9th grade algebra students. Provide 20 grade-appropriate problems, with an answer key on a separate page. At least three of the problems should be story problems. In the answer key, provide step-by-step reasoning for each solution.**

Not surprisingly, AI can help you grade your students' tests and homework. You might use a prompt like the following, after attaching a student's completed assignment:

**You are assisting me, a professor teaching a college-level introductory psychology course. Analyze and grade the attached student essay on abnormal psychology. Each essay should be at least 3 pages long and include at least 4 citations in MLA format. Don't be too picky about grammar and spelling, focus more on the content, whether it is appropriate and accurate. Provide constructive feedback, pointing out at least two strengths and one or more areas for improvement. Comment only, do not rewrite the essay.**

The key is to provide instructions to the AI similar to those you would provide to a teaching assistant helping you with the course. Spell out exactly what it is you want the AI to do, along with any content or other parameters specific to your course.

## Data Analysis and Research

Not surprisingly, AI is pretty good at analyzing data and doing research. All you have to do is feed it the appropriate data (typically by uploading a spreadsheet or database file) and tell it what you want to look at.

Your prompts should include the following parameters:

- Task/instructions
- Data or reference to data file
- Constraints (which part of the data to analyze, such as data from a set time period)
- Context (any additional info that could be of use)
- Audience
- Output format

Consider the task of analyzing sales data to identify key trends. You might construct a prompt like the following:

**Analyze the attached spreadsheet containing data on last fiscal year's sales by salesperson, region, and product line. Identify important trends and present in a one-page executive summary. Include a discussion of areas of opportunity moving forward.**

AI is also useful for explaining and summarizing complex data. Consider the following prompt:

**Analyze the attached file from the HR department. Summarize the employee data, focusing on demographic distributions (age, gender, location, and so on). We need to explain to upper management what our employee base looks like, using a short list of bullet points and a series of pie charts.**

Or, for your personal use, have AI analyze your household budget:

**The attached spreadsheet includes all our household expenses for the first six months of the year. Analyze our expenditures and put together a monthly budget for the rest of the year.**

Reference the applicable data, then tell AI what you want it to do with that data. Give it clear and concise instructions as far as what you want out of the data.

## Decision-Making

AI can go beyond analyzing data to using that analysis to assist in decision-making. Sometimes AI can see the one true path that might elude you otherwise.

When you want to use AI for decision-making, include the following parameters in your prompts:

- Problem to be solved or decision that must be made
- Data relevant to the decision
- Other context or considerations
- Constraints (things you absolutely cannot do)

Let's say, for example, you need to decide which of three potential new locations your company should open. You'd assemble relevant data on each location into one or more files, upload those files to the AI tool, and then enter the following prompt:

**Consider the attached files containing data about three possible store locations. We are considering opening one new store within the next six months. Analyze the data for each potential location and present a list of pros and cons for each location, in table format.**

You can then use that list of pros and cons to help make your decision. Or you can use that list to have AI make the decision for you, with the following prompt:

**Considering the list of pros and cons, with an emphasis on generating a working profit as quickly as possible while minimizing startup costs, recommend which new location we should open.**

You can also use AI for more personal decisions, such as determining where to spend your hard-earned money. Consider the following prompt:

**I just received a $5000 bonus. Our house is 23 years old and needs basic repairs. On the other hand, my wife and I haven't taken a vacation in three years. Should we spend the bonus on home repairs, such as repainting the house, or use the money for a well-earned vacation?**

AI will present the pros and cons of each option and hopefully lead you to the best decision.

## Summary

In this chapter, you learned some of the many ways you can use AI for productivity, and the types of prompts you can create. Know, however, that there's a lot more you can do with AI than is covered in this chapter; many work-related tasks use task-specific AI tools that have their own ways of doing things. Just remember, when you're using AI to assist with any productivity-related task, think of the AI as you would a human assistant and provide extremely detailed instructions.

Next up, you'll learn how to use prompt engineering to create better AI-generated images.

IN THIS CHAPTER

- Why create images with AI

- Discovering the best AI tools for image generation

- Key parameters for image generation prompts

- Examples of prompts for generating different types of images

- Best practices for AI image generation

18

# PROMPTING FOR IMAGE GENERATION

AI is becoming the go-to technology for generating all types of images. What used to be the purview of Adobe Photoshop and talented digital designers can now be done by anyone who knows how to feed a prompt into an AI image generator.

The key to creating great-looking images with AI is in the prompt. You have to accurately describe what it is you hope to see on the other side and convey those instructors to the AI image generator. As with all things AI, the better your prompt, the better your results—in this case, a (hopefully) great-looking picture of some sort.

**156** AI PROMPT ENGINEERING **ABSOLUTE BEGINNER'S GUIDE**

# Why Create Images with AI

In the old, old days of film photography, there was no way to create an image from scratch, other than enlisting the aid of an animation studio. Real-world images came from shooting your subject with a film camera, and then you could manipulate that film, to a slight degree, in the dark room—if you had your own dark room and knew how to use it.

When film photography was supplanted by digital photography, it became easier to manipulate the photos you took. Many online and software-based tools, such as Adobe Photoshop, were developed that let you edit digital images on a computer or smartphone. It wasn't necessarily creating new images from scratch, but it was a step beyond dodging and burning with photographic film.

> **NOTE** Dodging and burning were techniques used by film developers to lighten (dodge) or darken (burn) an area of a photographic image.

Photoshop and similar tools are now being superseded by AI image-generation tools. Using the same technologies as other AI tools, AI image generators let you tell the AI what type of image you want, and the AI will create it—seemingly out of thin air.

This ability to generate all types of images, from fantastic paintings to realistic photographs, makes it easy for anyone to become a digital artist. AI image generators can create new images, based on nothing more than your description, in a matter of seconds.

AI can create images that exist only in your imagination or that are indistinguishable from the real thing. AI can create images designed to look like oil paintings, charcoal sketches, crayon drawings, or high-end photographs. Most AI image generators are relatively easy to work with and cost little or nothing to use.

Why would you want to use an AI image generator? Here are just a few of the reasons:

- It's faster than drawing or creating something via conventional means. AI can generate an image that might take a human being hours or days in just seconds

- It's lower priced than using freelance artists or photographers—or purchasing stock photos

- It reduces or eliminates the need to hire professional graphic designers, illustrators, and photographers

- It lets you quickly and efficiently create a large number of images for social media, websites, marketing materials, and the like

- It enables non-artists (and non-photographers) to express themselves creatively and produce professional-looking results

- It's ideal for brainstorming and generating multiple possible images for consideration

- It lets you create mockups and visual representations of designs, products, and the like

- It lets you create photorealistic images of subjects and scenarios not possible in the real world

AI-generated images are already being used for both professional and personal applications. Businesses, especially marketing and advertising firms, are using AI-generated images to feed their other content, including blogs and advertisements. Individuals, like you and me, are creating AI-generated images for fun. And professional artists and graphic designers are using AI to help them brainstorm new ideas and generate first drafts for future projects.

When it comes to generating all types of images, AI is literally everywhere.

# Discovering the Best AI Tools for Image Generation

Many people don't realize that the major general AI tools can be used to generate images as well as text. In fact, these general AI tools have evolved into some of the best AI image generators. I'm talking about tools such as ChatGPT, Google Gemini, Grok, and Meta AI. You might want to make these tools your first stops when creating AI-generated images.

**NOTE**   Of the conventional AI tools, I've found Google Gemini to be among the best at image generation.

In addition, there are a number of AI tools designed specifically for image generation. These tools often feature interfaces and options that are specifically designed to make image generation easier. Table 18.1 details some of today's most popular dedicated image generators.

**TABLE 18.1**   Popular AI Image Generators

| AI Image Generator | URL |
| --- | --- |
| Adobe Firefly | www.adobe.com/firefly/ |
| Canva AI | www.canva.com/ai-image-generator |
| Craiyon | www.craiyon.com |
| Deep Dream Generator | www.deepdreamgenerator.com |
| DeepAI | www.deepai.org |
| Dreamstudio by Stability AI | dreamstudio.stability.ai |
| Flux Pro | www.flux1.ai/flux-pro |
| Hailuo AI | hailuoai.video |
| Hotpot | www.hotpot.ai |
| Ideogram | www.ideogram.ai |
| Microsoft Bing Image Creator | www.bing.com/images/create |
| Midjourney | www.midjourney.com |
| NightCafe | creator.nightcafe.studio |
| OpenArt | www.openart.ai |
| Sora | www.openai.com/sora/ |

# Key Parameters for Image Generation Prompts

When it comes to crafting an AI prompt designed to generate an image, the more descriptive you can be, the better. And there are a lot of ways you can describe any given image.

When you think about it, there are more variables involved in creating an image than there are in writing a piece of text. You have to decide what medium you're trying to recreate (photograph, painting, drawing, and so on), the style and mood of the image, the aspect ratio and resolution, and more. And that's before you start describing what is actually in the picture—the subject, the background, the composition, the lighting, you name it. You have to carefully consider all the various elements that make up an image and instruct the AI tool about each and every one of them.

To make it easier for you, take a look at Table 18.2, which details some of the more important image-related parameters you need to specify in your AI prompts. The more precisely you can describe what you want to see, the better your results will be.

**TABLE 18.2** Parameters for Image Generation Prompts

| Parameter | Description |
| --- | --- |
| Medium | What type of picture you're trying to emulate—photograph, oil painting, watercolor, digital art |
| Style | Artistic style within the medium—realistic, abstract, impressionistic |
| Subject/content | What is in the image—person, animal, object, landscape |
| Other objects | Other important people or objects in the picture |
| Details | Other specifics about the image—type of clothing, textures, facial expressions |
| Setting/environment | Where the picture is set |
| Lighting | Light source and direction—soft morning light, neon glow, candlelit |
| Color palette | Dominant color scheme—monochrome (black and white), pastels, vibrant colors, red hue |
| Mood/atmosphere | Emotional tone—cheerful, mysterious, pondering, romantic |
| Composition | How the picture should be composed—framing (close-up, portrait, wide shot), angle (from above, from below, eye level), and depth of field (shallow focus, blurred background) |
| Aspect ratio | Square, 4:3, 16:9, and so on |
| Resolution | Image quality, typically in pixels or other types of measurement |

# Examples of Prompts for Generating Different Types of Images

Writing an effective prompt for an AI image generator is more of an art than a science. You have to describe all the important elements in the image you want, while still allowing the AI some leeway in what it creates. And it's almost totally dependent on the prompts you create.

What does a prompt for AI image generation look like? Here are some examples, using the parameters previously presented:

**Create an expressionistic oil painting of a medieval castle on a rocky cliff overlooking a roiling sea below. The painting should be in a 4:3 aspect ratio.**

**FIGURE 18.1**

*Expressionistic oil painting, courtesy of Microsoft Bing Image Creator.*

**Give me a wide-angle photorealistic shot of a futuristic skyscraper in the bright midday sun, with dirigibles flying about. Make it brightly colored.**

**Generate an aerial drone view of a tropical island with a sandy beach and turquoise waters, in 16:9 ratio with realistic photography.**

**FIGURE 18.2**

*Photorealistic aerial view of a tropical island, courtesy of Meta AI.*

Draw a crayon illustration of a butterfly flying through a rainbow, in the style of a six year-old, as if drawn on a brown paper bag.

Create a close-up black and white photograph of an elderly fisherman with deep wrinkles, wearing a dark cap and peacoat.

**FIGURE 18.3**

*Black and white photo of an old fisherman, courtesy of Google Gemini.*

Generate a 16:9 aspect ratio photo of a saltwater fish tank, complete with clown fish, yellow tangs, a Picasso triggerfish, and multicolored corals, with light from above shimmering through the water.

Give me a cartoonish image of a baby tiger riding a bicycle through a park as various other anthropomorphic animals look on.

**FIGURE 18.4**

*A baby tiger riding a bicycle, courtesy of Dreamstudio by Stability AI.*

Create a watercolor painting of a desert canyon at sunset, with warm orange and purple tones. Make it an ultrawide panoramic image.

Generate a photograph of a woman in her mid-thirties with long red hair, pale skin, freckles, and pale blue eyes, wearing a white blouse with minimal makeup, staring out a window, lit exclusively by the light from the window.

**FIGURE 18.5**

*A photographic portrait of a redheaded woman, courtesy of Midjourney.*

Create a photorealistic image of a tiny mouse sitting at a computer under a mushroom, typing at the computer keyboard as his tutor looks over his shoulder.

Generate a close-up studio shot of a delicious salad with vibrant greens and colorful vegetables. Include a blurry kitchen background with shallow depth of field, in 4K resolution.

**FIGURE 18.6**

*A delicious and colorful salad, courtesy of Adobe Firefly.*

Create a vibrant collage using torn cutout images of vintage automobiles. Make it a square image suitable for framing.

Create a charcoal sketch of a knight in shining armor battling a fire-breathing dragon

**FIGURE 18.7**

*A charcoal sketch of a knight battling a dragon, courtesy of OpenArt.*

Create a high contrast black-and-white photograph of an old-growth forest, in portrait mode, in the style of Ansel Adams.

Create a whimsical 3D illustration of a set of dancing colored pencils, each color with its own distinct personality. They should be dancing in front of their pencil box on a tabletop, with the giant face of an excited child watching them in the background.

**FIGURE 18.8**

*3D dancing colored pencils, courtesy of Craiyon.*

Finally, many AI tools let you upload your own image files that you can use to create new images. For example, you can upload a picture of yourself and ask AI to turn you into a pro football player on the field, or turn a casual photo into a professional-looking headshot you can use on a resume:

**Use the attached photo of me and turn it into a professional headshot. Have me wearing a suit and tie and trim my hair and beard.**

**FIGURE 18.9**

*An AI-generated headshot of the author, courtesy of Google Gemini. (I don't look near that good, normally.)*

Try these prompts—and more of your own—on your favorite AI image generator and see what you get!

# Best Practices for AI Image Generation

Crafting the perfect prompt to generate perfect images is just like crafting a text prompt for an all-purpose AI tool, but with visual concerns added. It's really about describing exactly what you want to see—the main image, the background, the style, the output type, and more.

When crafting a prompt for image generation, then, follow these best practices:

- **Be as specific as possible.** Don't use empty words that have a low information content, such as "beautiful" or "wonderful." Use specific adjectives to describe appearance, mood, style, and other details. Instead of asking for a picture of "a dog," ask instead for "a fluffy golden retriever puppy."

- **Use adjectives.** Add descriptive words to control the look and feel of the image, such as "a weathered, ornate treasure chest."

- **Include motion and emotion.** Don't just describe who or what is in the picture, but what they're doing. Instead of saying "children on a playground," say instead, "children chasing each other around a playground." Instead of saying "a couple looking at each other," say a "couple looking lovingly at each other."

- **If there's a style you want to emulate, point it out.** If you want a picture in the style of Van Gogh or Norman Rockwell, include that in your prompt. If it's a photo you want, say you want a photo or even a specific type of photo, like an Annie Leibovitz portrait or an Ansel Adams landscape.

- **If you want someone or something real in the image, say so.** Instead of saying you want a picture of a beach, say you want "a picture of Pacific Beach in California." If you want a picture to look like someone famous, say so, like "a picture of a rancher who looks like Robert Redford."

- **Mention relevant technical terms.** Think like an artist or photographer. For example, when creating photorealistic images, use terms like *8K*, *4K*, *macro shot*, *wide angle*, *cinematic lighting*, or *bokeh*.

- **Use the options available for the AI tool.** Some AI image generation tools only let you input a text prompt. Others include various controls and options that help you fine-tune your image. If there are options available, use them.

Remember, different AI image generators will generate different images. You may need to try several different tools to get the results you want. And don't be afraid to fine-tune your query or "remix" an image if the first one you get is close but not quite right. When generating AI images, experimentation is key.

> **NOTE** As good as most AI tools are at generating images, some have trouble generating any text within an image—a newspaper headline, for example, or a street sign. If a given AI tool can't generate proper text, try your prompt with a different tool that may produce better results.

# HOW TO USE AI-GENERATED IMAGES ETHICALLY

While generating images with AI can be fun, you need to be cautious about how you use those AI-generated images. You shouldn't claim an AI-generated image as something you've created yourself, you shouldn't use it to fool people, and you have to be careful about appropriating any copyrighted images.

Keep the following in mind:

- **Don't claim credit.** The art generated by AI is not art that you personally create. Some artists have gotten into trouble trying to pass off AI-generated artwork as their own creations. It's not.

- **Don't claim copyright.** You can't copyright artwork that you didn't create yourself. Period.

- **Be transparent.** If you're presenting AI-generated artwork, let people know that it's AI-generated artwork. A simple credit line or caption along the lines of "Generated by AI" or "AI-generated art" will let people know what they're actually seeing.

- **Don't pass off AI-generated art as real.** AI can generate photorealistic images. Don't try to fool people into thinking they're real images. As before, be transparent and let people know the images were AI generated.

- **Don't use copyrighted images.** When creating images with AI, be careful not to infringe on any copyrights. That means don't create images of copyrighted characters, and don't use images that are clearly based on copyrighted material.

- **Don't create deepfakes.** Using AI to create images of real people in less-than-real situations is not only unethical but also may be illegal. Don't use AI as propaganda, to misinform, or to spread false information. You should never use AI to try to fool people in any way, shape, or form.

Bottom line, you shouldn't use AI-generated images to fool people and you shouldn't fool them into thinking that AI-generated art is real. Be honest about what you're doing but be responsible about how you do it.

## Summary

In this chapter, you learned how to create effective prompts for AI-generated images. If you include the appropriate instructions and information in your prompt, you can generate almost any type of image imaginable—from realistic photographs to wildly imaginative fantasies.

And that's how you generate still images. In the next chapter, we'll look at moving images—how to use AI to generate movies and videos.

## IN THIS CHAPTER

- Why create videos with AI
- Discovering the best AI tools for generating videos
- Key parameters for video generation prompts
- Examples of prompts for generating different types of videos
- Best practices for AI video generation
- Pitfalls inherent in AI video generation

# 19

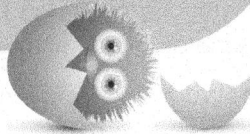

# PROMPTING FOR VIDEO GENERATION

The field of AI video generation is advancing rapidly. What used to be only a pipedream is today an assemblage of tools that you can use to generate highly realistic videos in a matter of seconds.

These AI video generators let anyone become a movie director—without having to buy expensive lighting and camera equipment or hire equally expensive (and often temperamental) actors. All you have to do is describe to AI the video that you want to create, and it will do it to the best of its (constantly evolving) capability.

# Why Create Videos with AI

Creating AI-generated videos for your own personal use can be fun. For filmmakers and would-be filmmakers, it can enhance and ease the creative process. For businesses, it can be a less-expensive alternative to professional video creation.

In short, Ai video generation offers something for everyone.

Depending on your needs or intentions, AI-generated video offers

- **Speed and efficiency:** AI can do in minutes what it takes days or weeks to do with traditional video production methods.

- **Lower costs:** While AI video generation isn't free, it's much less costly than obtaining expensive cameras, lights, actors, and crews.

- **Ease of production:** You don't have to rent an expensive studio or transport a whole crew to a remote location. You can generate AI videos from the comfort of your desk or living room, using your desktop or laptop computer.

- **Accessibility:** You don't need filmmaking skills or experience to make AI videos. With AI video generation, anybody and everybody can be filmmakers.

- **Personalization at scale**. For businesses, AI makes it easy to create custom videos for specific audiences, including personalized ads, training modules, and the like.

- **Creative possibilities**. With AI, you're not limited to shooting the real world through a camera lens. AI lets you create visuals that would be impossible to film or extremely expensive to generate with CGI, including historical locales, fantasy worlds, futuristic cities, and the like.

While AI is unlikely to completely replace human filmmakers (although it might...), it lets both pros and amateurs focus on their creativity while it handles a lot of the behind-the-scenes heavy lifting. Just enter your instructions into a prompt box and let AI create the videos of your dreams.

# Discovering the Best AI Tools for Generating Videos

There are a number of AI video generators available to the public (most priced on a subscription basis), with more being introduced on a regular basis. This is an area where advancements are coming fast and furious, with performance improving dramatically from version to version.

That said, you should check out any of these tools before investing in a (sometimes expensive) subscription. You should also know that you may need to take several runs at any given prompt to get the results you want, which uses up any credits you might have in a subscription.

In other words, be prepared to spend some real money if you're serious about generating AI videos. And remember, you'll get much different results from each of these tools, so trying a prompt on multiple tools is more the norm than the exception.

Take a look at some of the most popular current AI video generators in Table 19.1.

**TABLE 19.1**   Popular AI Video Generators

| AI Video Generator | URL |
| --- | --- |
| Adobe Firefly | www.adobe.com/firefly |
| DeepAI | www.deepai.org |
| Dream Machine | dream-machine.lumalabs.ai |
| Fotor | www.fotor.com/apps/ai-video-generator |
| Google Veo | labs.google/flow/about (via Google Flow) or gemini.google.com (via Google Gemini Pro) |
| Hailuoai | hailuoai.video |
| KlingAI | www.klingai.com |
| Luma Dream Machine | www.lumalabs.ai/dream-machine |
| Runway | www.runwayml.com |
| Seedance | www.seedance.ai |
| Sora | www.openai.com/sora |
| Vidu | www.vidu.com |

As noted, you're not going to get much in the way of AI video generation for free. While some of these tools might offer a limited amount of free or trial use, you'll need to pony up for a subscription to do any serious video generation at all—and some of these subscriptions are pricey. Video generation uses up a lot of resources, and those resources have to be paid for, so have your credit card handy!

**NOTE**   As of this writing, most of these consumer-oriented AI video generation tools only let you produce short (6 to 12 seconds) and silent videos. Few generate audio to accompany the video.

# Key Parameters for Video Generation Prompts

When generating AI videos, it's important that your prompts completely describe the scene, the subject(s), the camera movements, and all the technical details, including aspect ratio, frame rate, and the like. You have to think like a director and include all the necessary directors to all the actors and technical crew (all played by AI, of course).

Table 19.2 details some of the most important parameters to include when crafting prompts for video generation. You can use some or all of these parameters in your prompts, as appropriate, but the more descriptive you are, the better.

**TABLE 19.2**  Parameters for Video Generation Prompts

| Parameter | Description |
| --- | --- |
| Subject/scene | What the video is about |
| Setting/background | The location and context, in detail |
| Characters | Characters in the scene—what they look like, their motivations, how they act |
| Action | What happens in the video, motion cues |
| Camera motion | Static, panning, zooming, and so forth |
| Genre | Documentary, mystery, rom-com, horror |
| Visual style | Realistic, cartoonish |
| Mood/tone | Peaceful, romantic, suspenseful |
| Lighting | Natural, dramatic, soft, and so forth |
| Color palette/grading | Warm tones, pastel, high contrast, black and white |
| Audio | If the AI tool generates audio (not all do), select ambient audio, narration, dialogue (detailed for different actors) sound effects, type of music, and the like |
| Aspect ratio | 16:9, 4:3, square |
| Resolution | 720p, 1080p, 4K |
| Frame rate | Frames per second (FPS) |
| Length | In seconds or minutes |

Include as many or as few of these parameters in your prompts as necessary. As with all things AI, the more detailed your instructions, the better the results.

# Examples of Prompts for Generating Different Types of Videos

What does a prompt for an AI video look like? Well, this type of prompt is typically more involved than a prompt for text content or image creation. That's because there's a lot going on in a video—what you see and hear, the action that develops, how the subjects act, and such. You also have to describe what happens behind the camera—all the technical details, lighting, camera movements and the like.

To get an idea of what a video generation prompt might look like, consider the following examples. Each of these prompts incorporates many of the parameters just discussed, in a clear and concise fashion.

Here are the prompts:

**Create a 12-second nature video in 16:9 aspect ratio, 1080p resolution, and 24 fps frame rate. This should be one continuous shot as a drone flies over lush green fields and rolling hills somewhere in Ireland. The camera zooms along a dirt path as the drone approaches a cliff far above a rocky beach. Golden sunlight glimmers on the water below. Ultra-realistic style, National Geographic documentary feel, with gentle Irish background music.**

**Generate a 15-second video in 16:9, 4K, 30 fps. We see a futuristic city skyline at night, filled with flying cars and brightly colored neon signs. The camera glides between towering skyscrapers, reflecting neon light on glass surfaces. Cyberpunk style, moody atmosphere, Blade Runner vibes.**

**Create a 6-second looping video in square aspect ratio, 720p, 12 fps, for use in social media posts. A cartoon-style cat chases a red ball of yarn around a plain white room filled with colorful furniture and other objects. The flat animation should be bright, colorful, and playful, in the style of a Saturday morning cartoon.**

**Generate a short video in cinematic, 35mm film style, highly detailed, shallow depth of field. We're in a barren and snowy landscape with gray clouds in the sky and snow-covered mountains in the distance. Start with a wide shot, slowly zooming in on a large polar bear with bright white fur walking slowly but confidently toward a hole in the ice. He stops and peers down inquisitively into the hole. Nature sounds on the soundtrack.**

**Generate a 10-second vertical video in 9:16 ratio, 1080p, 30 fps. Picture brightly colored flowing 3D liquid shapes against a jet-black background. Vibrant neon colors pulse to the rhythm of an electronic soundtrack. Abstract, trippy, and surreal.**

Create a 12-second 4:3 ratio video, 1080p resolution, 24 fps. Black and white cinematography, film noir style. The scene: A rain dampened city street at night with fog rolling in. Two characters, Lew Marlowe and Bridgette Shaw. Lew is in a trench coat and 1940s style hat, Bridgette is wearing a dark dress and era-appropriate hat. They are staring at each other, about to embrace. The camera starts in a long shot and slowly zooms into their faces. We fade out as they kiss.

Create a short widescreen video in high resolution of an astronaut floating outside a space station, Earth in the background, with zero-gravity movements and realistic physics. The camera should be moving from left to right around the astronaut. Include realistic conversation between the astronaut and mission control.

Create a cinematic 15-second video in 16:9, 1080p, 24 fps. Setting is a modern city street at sunset, with skyscrapers looming overhead, lit orange by the setting sun. A soldier in black body armor carrying a high-tech weapon battles a giant mechanical robot that stands a half-dozen stories high. The robot stomps relentlessly through the city toward the soldier, smashing cars and fire hydrants underneath its giant metallic feet. The camera, positioned behind the soldier, pans upward from the soldier to take on the enormity of the giant robot as sparks and smoke fill the air. Epic, realistic style with dramatic golden lighting.

Generate a short 16:9 aspect ratio video based on the attached photo of me. I should be walking and talking, with the following dialog: "Hello, there. As you can see, AI can literally put words into my mouth and make it look extremely realistic."

> **NOTE** Not all AI image generators can also generate audio, especially spoken dialog. For those that do, you'll need to specify the words you want spoken—or some direction as to what the dialog should be.

What you see in common across all these prompts is a listing of specific technical details, accompanied by a detailed scene description and instructions for camera movements. This is what any AI video generator needs in order to create the videos you want.

# Best Practices for AI Video Generation

When moving into AI video generation, keep these best practices in mind to get the best results:

- **Structure your prompt for clarity:** Put your technical specs in a separate sentence or section than your scene setting, camera directions, and such. Read through the prompt to ensure that a human director would understand what you're asking for; if you're confused, AI likely will be, too.

- **Be specific and descriptive:** Include as many details as necessary; don't assume the AI will just know what you want. Avoid general or abstract language and don't be ambiguous. Use precise and descriptive words in your instructions.

- **Focus on a single, simple action:** Since videos created by today's AI video generators are still limited in length, don't try to tell an overly complex story in a single prompt. Keep the action clear and simple.

- **Include camera and lighting instructions:** Think like a director and include directions in terms of camera angles and movements, as well as lighting and other scene details.

- **Iterate and refine:** Even though video generation is more expensive per minute than other AI-related tasks, get used to rerunning a prompt (either exactly or with modifications) to fine-tune your results. You will likely need to run a prompt multiple times, refining the prompt as you go, to get acceptable results.

- **Reference appropriate styles and genres:** Unless you're going for something totally fantastic and unique, give the AI appropriate guidance by referencing similar styles, genres, or content. This gives the AI a starting point when creating the video.

- **Define your goal and audience:** Let the AI know if you're creating a video for social media (TikTok, YouTube, and so on), for a business presentation, or whatever.

- **Incorporate negative prompts:** Some (but not all) AI tools let you specify things to exclude from your videos, typically by using a minus sign (–) in front of what you don't want. So, for example, if you want to exclude painting on a wall, enter **–no paintings**; if you don't want to be overly salacious, enter **–bare skin**. You get the point.

Remember, AI video generation is in its relative infancy. Be prepared for lots of hiccups, but also for the video generation tools to get a whole lot better pretty fast.

> **NOTE**   One of the primary dangers of AI-generated video involves the creation of *deepfakes*—videos of people doing or saying things they never would in real life. As AI-generated videos continue to evolve and look more realistic, it will become easier to fool people into thinking that a fake video is actually real. This is likely to result in the spread of disinformation and cause people to distrust even real videos if they can't tell what's fake or not.

# Pitfalls Inherent in AI Video Generation

Because of the complexity involved, AI-generated video is one of the most problematic types of AI-generated content. You'll get better and more consistent results generating text and images than you will creating even short AI-generated videos.

In particular, be aware of these things:

- Lack of consistency, with characters or objects changing appearance from frame to frame
- Distorted body and hands (fingers especially)
- No or slow blinking
- Physics that don't make sense
- Lack of gravity—characters seemingly standing in or walking on air
- Difficulty generating readable text
- Difficulty rendering fine details
- Poor lip syncing (for those models that offer audio)
- Background sounds mismatched to the video (such as nature sounds behind a city street scene)

In addition, know that AI-generated videos can exhibit the same biases as other forms of AI-generated content. Unless you specify otherwise, characters in your videos are likely to be white and male and possibly exhibit other societal biases. Work hard to specify details that fight against these biases and present your true, hopefully nonbiased vision.

You should also know that today's video generation tools are somewhat limited in what they can produce. Most of these tools are limited to relatively short videos, typically just a few seconds long. And many of these tools generate only video, not sound. That means you can't yet use AI to generate a complete movie, or even a 60-second commercial. The cost of producing AI video is just too high—right now—to create longer works. It's fun to play with, but things will need to change before you can create longer audio/video content with AI.

The bottom line is that you need to check and double-check the videos you generate with AI and be prepared to run each prompt multiple times. As you will quickly realize, AI video generation is still imperfect—which means that human oversight is essential.

## Summary

In this chapter, you learned how to craft detailed prompts for AI-generated video, including the most important parameters to include. There's a lot involved in creating AI videos, so be prepared for a lot of work.

The next chapter moves on to audio and how to write effective prompts for generating music.

## IN THIS CHAPTER

- Why use AI to generate music
- Discovering the best AI tools for creating music
- Key parameters for music generation prompts
- Examples of prompts to generate different types of music
- Creating lyrics

20

# PROMPTING FOR MUSIC GENERATION

Did you know that AI can write songs? It's true, AI music generation tools let you create all types of music, just by entering a few words into a prompt.

It's not quite that easy, however. You need to know what parameters to include in your prompts and what tools to use. When you get into it, however, you might be surprised at how good AI-generated music can be—in many cases, indistinguishable from music created by real-life artists.

# Why Use AI to Generate Music

For many musicians, writing music is an inherently personal endeavor. Many artists pour their hearts and souls into their songs, crafting melodies that lift their lyrics into the hearts and minds of their listeners.

For many companies, however, music is a necessary and sometimes expensive evil. Consider companies that supply the background music you hear when you're on hold or waiting in the dentist's office. The money they pay to musicians to write and record that music is just another expense in the ledger book.

For those companies, the ability to use AI to generate music, for low or no cost, is a very good thing. AI music generation tools have advanced to the point where casual listeners cannot tell AI-generated music—including AI-generated vocals—from the real thing.

Consider these possible reasons to use an AI music generator to create songs and music of all types:

- Businesses, such as music on-hold companies, can use AI to generate background music at a considerably lower cost than music created by musicians.

- Streaming music services can use AI-generated music to fill out listener playlists with music on which they don't have to pay royalties, thus cutting costs.

- Marketers and advertisers can use AI to generate jingles and background music for commercials, at a lower cost than employing traditional musicians.

- Musicians can use AI to provide inspiration, flesh out existing ideas, and fine-tune their music—essentially acting as collaborators in their art.

- Musicians can also use AI to create practice tracks and demos, as well as create complete arrangements and orchestrations.

- Nonmusicians can use AI to create their own music, even if they've never read or played a note in their lives.

- Other creatives can use AI to generate background music and soundtracks for podcasts, YouTube and TikTok videos, video games, short films, and more.

So, yes, artificial intelligence can replace flesh and blood musicians for many applications, but it can also expand musicians' toolkits. In addition, AI opens up the world of music creation to people who aren't trained musicians.

# Discovering the Best AI Tools for Creating Music

Most general AI tools, like ChatGPT and Grok, are not designed to create music. Instead, you need to use a dedicated AI music generator built with the algorithms necessary to generate music of all types.

These AI music generators are designed specifically for music creation. To create a piece of music, you simply enter a prompt that describes the type of tune you'd like to create. Interfaces typically include a prompt box with options for different types of music, as well as a lyric editor to add your own or generate new lyrics. (Figure 20.1 shows the Suno AI music generator.)

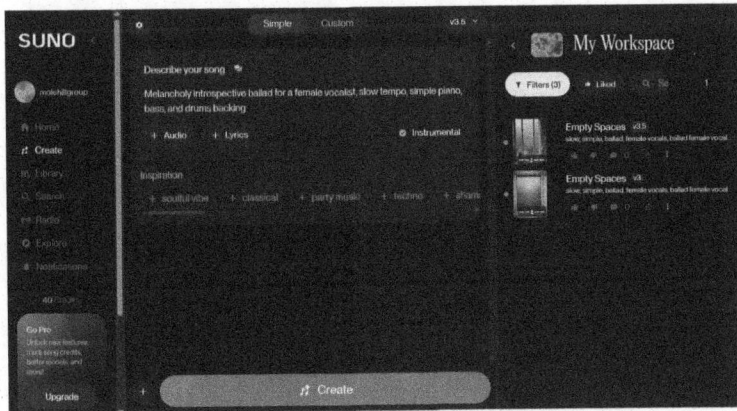

**FIGURE 20.1**

*Creating music with Suno.*

The tunes you've created typically appear in a separate library or workspace pane. Click to open the page for any particular song; then you can play, download, or share the music you've created. (Figure 20.2 shows a newly created song in Suno.)

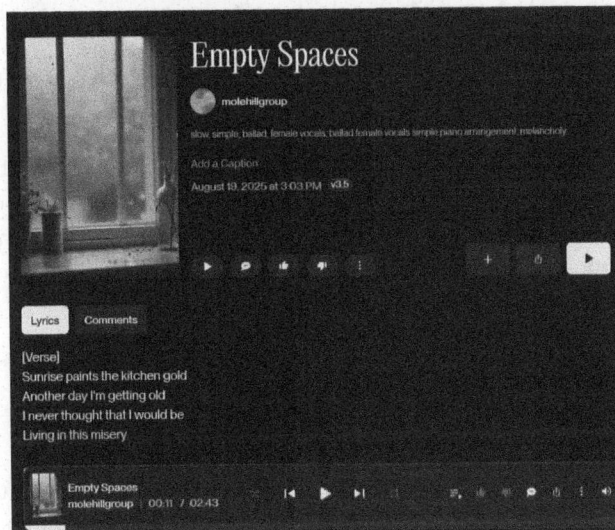

**FIGURE 20.2**

*An AI-generated song in Suno.*

Table 20.1 details some of the most popular AI music generators today.

**TABLE 20.1**   Popular AI Music Generators

| AI Music Generator | URL |
| --- | --- |
| AIVA | www.aiva.ai |
| Beatoven | www.beatoven.ai |
| Boomy | www.boomy.com |
| Choruz | www.choruz.ai |
| Loudly | www.loudly.com |
| Mureka | www.mureka.ai |
| RiffGen | www.riffgen.com |
| Soundful | www.soundful.com |
| Soundraw | www.soundraw.io |
| Suno | www.suno.com |
| Udio | www.udio.com |

**NOTE**   Most AI music generators let you create either a set number of tunes or shortened versions of tunes (typically 30 seconds or so long) for free, but they require a subscription to generate full tunes at the best audio quality.

All of these AI music generators work in a similar fashion. You enter a text prompt with the necessary parameters, select whatever options might be available, and then click the Create button. The AI then generates one or more pieces of music that match the prompt's requirements. You can then listen to the generated music, share it with others, or download it for your own use.

Know, however, that the resulting music can be wildly different from tool to tool; some are more creative, some generate higher-quality files, some aren't as flexible or as understanding of complex prompts and parameters. AI music generation is definitely one area where it pays to try out multiple competitors to find the one that best suits your needs.

# Key Parameters for Music Generation Prompts

In general, the more you tell an AI tool about the music you want to generate, the closer it will get to what you want. Give it a rather vague and generic prompt, such as **write me a love song**, and who knows what you'll get—it could be an uptempo country tune, a hard rock power ballad, or a sensitive acoustic guitar-driven lament. You need to specify all the pertinent details about the song to get the best results—parameters like genre, style or tone, tempo, dynamics, instrumentation, topic, male or female singer, and the like.

Now, a trained musician might know all of this already and be able to create a detailed prompt in less than a minute. Those of you who aren't trained musicians need only walk through the optional parameters detailed in Table 20.2. If you don't know or care about a particular parameter, leave it out. If you don't know specifics about a given parameter, such as genre or song form, do your best to describe it. But enter as much about a piece of music as you know in advance.

**TABLE 20.2** Parameters for Music Generation Prompts

| Parameter | Description |
|---|---|
| Title | If you have a specific title in mind, enter it (in quotation marks); if not, let the AI tool generate a title. |
| Topic or content | What the song is about; if you want to mention any specify people or items to be included in the song (such as beer and pickup trucks in a country song), do so. |
| Intended audience | Who or what you're creating this for, such as teen girls, dance clubs, top 40 radio, and the like. |
| Genre | Describe the genre you're writing for, such as country, rock, and hip hop. |
| Style | Within a genre, the specific characteristics of the music; think of it as a sub-genre, such as prog rock, cool jazz, or gangsta rap. |
| Song type | Within a genre or style, the type of work you want to create, such as ballads, anthems, love songs, party songs, and the like. |
| Mood/emotion | Describe the feeling you wish to convey, such as sad, inspiring, dreamy, or angry. |
| Rhythm/groove | The rhythmic feel or pattern, such as straight-ahead, syncopated, or funky. |
| Tempo | How fast the song is; you can specify the exact beats per minute (bpm) or a general speed, such as slow, midtempo, uptempo, and the like. |
| Dynamics | How loud or soft the music should be; you can specify exact musical dynamics (pianissimo, forte) or just say soft, loud, moderately loud, and the like. |
| Time signature | 4/4, 3/4, 6/8, and the like. |
| Key signature | What key you want the music to be in (include major or minor). |
| Melodic range | The range of the melody, either generally (wide range, narrow range), in intervals (a full octave, an octave in a third), specific notes (middle C to the G above the treble clef staff). |
| Harmonic quality | The quality of the chords and melody; how often the chords should change, what types of chords (simple triads, power chords, extended chords), and so on. |
| Song structure | The construction of the song, such as 12-bar blues; verse-chorus-verse; two verses, a chorus, and a bridge. |

| Parameter | Description |
|---|---|
| Instrumentation | What instruments you want in the piece; either a general description (rhythm section with horns, four-piece rock band) or specify particular instruments (2 trumpets, 1 trombone, cello). |
| Singer | Male or female, voice quality (raspy, breathy), type of voice (soprano, alto, tenor, bass). |
| Length | How long the piece should be; you can leave the length up to the AI, specify a general length, or specify an exact length in minutes and seconds. |
| Examples | If you want the music to be in the style of a particular artist or period, specify that (such as **a pop song like Taylor Swift** or **like a Duke Ellington big band piece**). |

Combine some or all of these parameters in a single prompt to generate the desired piece of music.

> **NOTE**   Some AI music generators won't let you reference specific artists in a prompt. So, you couldn't ask it to write a song like Taylor Swift, but you could ask it to write a teen country-pop breakup song.

# Examples of Prompts to Generate Different Types of Music

Construct a prompt to generate a piece of music, then, involves specifying as many parameters as possible or necessary. Entering **create a catchy pop song** isn't enough; you also need to specify important information about that uptempo dance song.

Here are some examples of prompts to generate specific pieces of music:

**Write a midtempo good ol' boy country song for a male singer about things like bros, boots, beers, girls in cutoff jeans, and pickup trucks. Make sure you include a slide guitar and fiddle, and make sure the vocal range is no more than an octave.**

**Write a dreamy instrumental electropop dance tune, 120 bpm, to play in a dance lounge**

**Give me an East Coast hip-hop track with a gritty, urban vibe, 90 bpm. Use sampled jazz piano chords, boom-bap drums, and a deep bassline. The words should focus on persevering in tough environments. Structure it with an intro, verses, choruses, and a short outro, no more than 5 minutes long.**

Write a new wave song for a band with 2 guitars, synth, bass, and drums. Fast tempo, female singer with limited vocal range, drums with kind of a disco beat. Include the lyrics "Watch for the new world." Give it kind of a detached but angry vibe.

Write a classic rock guitar song for a four-piece band with a male singer, loud and fast shuffle beat, about traveling down the highway, should appeal to a slightly older audience who likes CCR and the Rolling Stones

Write an uptempo song about breaking up with my boyfriend, kind of confessional pop, with a strong hook and a sing-along chorus, give it a glossy production with lots of synths and electronics

Create a prog rock song, lots of synths and strings, in 5/4 time, titled "The World Beyond," about technology and the future, about 6 minutes long, include an instrumental section in the middle with dueling synth and lead guitar, high vocal range for a strong male voice (think Robert Plant) and fast fusion drumming (think Neal Peart)

Write a simple sing-songy children's tune about the colors of the rainbow, make it easily singable by grade school kids, just a verse with no chorus, about a half minute long, and have it sung by a small children's chorus

Create an inoffensive new age instrumental piece, in the Windham Hill style, with mellow acoustic piano, cello, and flute, something that can seamlessly repeat, for use as background on-hold music for a telephone system

Write a 15-second jingle for a commercial for Honest Bob's, a used-car dealer, with catchy hook sung by a mixed chorus, ("Honest Bob's Has Honest Deals"), straight uptempo beat, bright and chirpy but suitable for play on an easy listening station

Create the theme music for a podcast, 20 seconds long, fast tempo and a driving beat with lots of electric guitars, strong rhythmic pulse

Write a fast swing number for big band, 160 bpm, in the key of F, starting soft and building to a fortissimo middle section, then include a section for solos, then back to the main theme for the ending, employ sophisticated harmonies and extended chords

Create a string quartet in the Romantic style, in 3/4 time, moderate tempo, in the key of E minor, in the style of Beethoven, broadly melodic, approximately 5 minutes long

# Creating Lyrics

Most AI music generators can generate both music and words, but that doesn't mean that's the way to go. You may want to write the words yourself and let the AI set them to music. Or you may want to generate lyrics with a different AI tool, such as ChatGPT or Google Gemini and then have the AI music tool set them to music.

To this end, some AI music generators have an option to enter your own lyrics. (In Udio, for example, this is called the Lyric Editor, as shown in Figure 20.3.) You can either manually enter your lyrics or paste lyrics you've created and cut from another source.

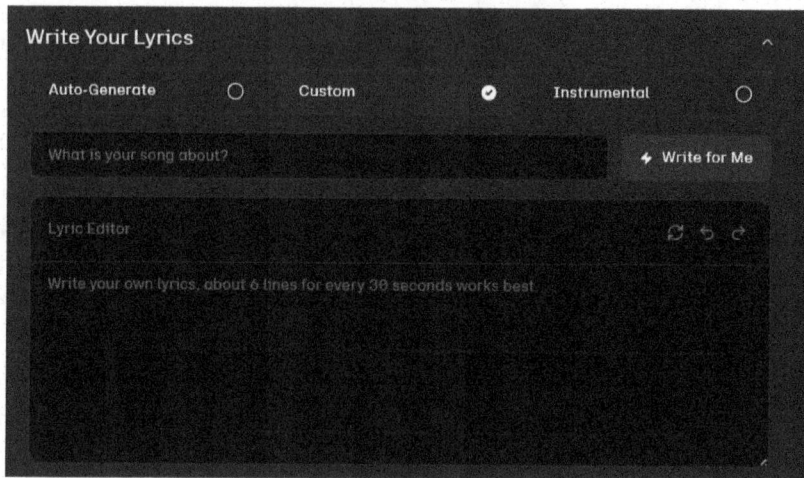

**FIGURE 20.3**

*Udio's Lyric Editor, for entering your own lyrics.*

When you're using a lyric editor, you can use headings or tags such as [Verse] or [Chorus] to delineate specific sections of the song, as shown in Figure 20.4. Some lyric editors even let you enter partial lyrics and let the music generator flesh out the rest.

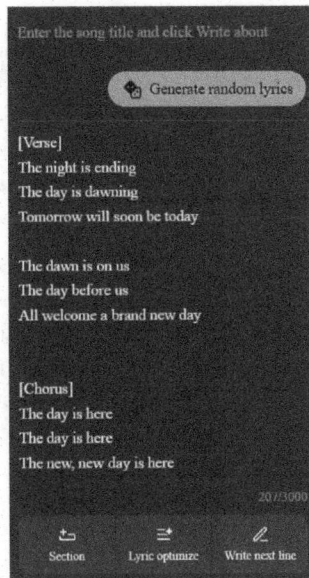

Enter the song title and click Write about

Generate random lyrics

[Verse]
The night is ending
The day is dawning
Tomorrow will soon be today

The dawn is on us
The day before us
All welcome a brand new day

[Chorus]
The day is here
The day is here
The new, new day is here

207/3000

Section    Lyric optimize    Write next line

**FIGURE 20.4**

*Lyrics in Mureka with [Verse] and [Chorus] sections.*

# THE ETHICS OF AI-GENERATED MUSIC

While some musicians are using AI to assist their creative processes and many large companies are embracing AI as a way to obtain cheap (or free) music for various purposes, not everyone is a fan of AI-generated music.

First, there's the whole concept of using inexpensive AI tools to create music that replaces music made by human musicians. That can be a huge cost-saver for a company like Spotify, which seeds user playlists with AI-generated tracks that sound similar to user-selected music but doesn't require them to pay royalties. Casual listeners might not notice the faux music, but more discerning music lovers might be appalled or offended by the attempt to pass off machine music as the real thing.

Even worse is when a creator tries to pass off AI-generated music and AI-generated "artists" as the real thing. A recent controversy arose when The Velvet Sundown, a relatively new band who'd released several albums in a short period of time, was revealed to be completely AI-generated—the band's "members," their photos, their background info, and, of course, their music, was all conjured up by artificial intelligence tools.

Then there's the issue of using AI to generate background music for use in on-hold phone systems, elevators, and the like. Does it really matter if the annoying music you hear when you're put on hold is generated by real musicians or by an AI tool? It certainly matters to those musicians who used to record these tracks and are now out of work, but for those of us forced to listen to this stuff while we're (im)patiently waiting on hold, who cares where it comes from?

The ultimate question here, musicians' incomes aside, is whether artificial intelligence can generate truly creative art. Is it possible that, at some time in the future, we'll hear AI tunes with the same soul, wit, and insight as songs by Bob Dylan, the Beatles, or Taylor Swift? As a musician myself, the concept of AI-generated music is inherently offensive. That said, it may be good enough for casual listeners—and, if that's the case, what's wrong with that?

## Summary

In this chapter, you learned how to create prompts for use with AI music generators. You learned about the most popular AI music generation tools and the most important parameters to use in your prompts. These tools work surprisingly well and can generate music that, to casual listeners, is indistinguishable from that created by flesh-and-blood musicians.

Next up, it's time to learn some advanced prompting techniques—as well as discover tools you can use to create and fine-tune your prompts.

# 21

# ADVANCED PROMPTING STRATEGIES AND TOOLS

If you've gotten this far in this book, you've already learned some advanced prompting techniques. Just about anything beyond zero-shot prompting is technically an advanced strategy, so if you're using one-shot, role-based, chain-of-thought, or self-consistency prompting, you're already an advanced AI prompt engineer.

That said, there's always more you can do with your prompts to make them even more effective. That's what you'll learn in this chapter—how to employ more advanced prompting strategies and how to use freestanding prompting tools.

# Advanced Prompt Engineering Techniques

When you want to take your prompt engineering to the next level, you can augment your prompts with some of the following techniques. Not all are suitable for all types of prompts, and all involve a level of difficulty somewhat beyond normal prompting, but you may find the results worth the effort.

## Structured Prompting

Structured prompting is one of the simplest advanced techniques, and one you may already be using. It involves breaking up long prompts into easily identified sections. You can use headings, bullet lists, tables, and delimiters to separate and identify separate pieces of information within a prompt.

**NOTE** A delimiter is any character used to separate sections in a prompt or surround key information in a prompt. Separating delimiters can include dashes, asterisks, and other symbols; surrounding delimiters can include quotes, brackets, and other similar characters.

For example, you might want to add the header **TASK** before defining the task in the prompt, the header **CONTEXT** before any background information, and the header **OUTPUT FORMAT** before defining the desired format of the output.

Structuring your prompts in this manner helps clarify the instructions you provide to the AI. Just as this type of visual organization can improve readability for human readers, it can also help AI "see" and better understand the separate components of a complex prompt.

## Prompt Decomposition

Similar to structured prompting is the technique of prompt decomposition. This is just a fancy way of saying that you break complex tasks into shorter, more manageable substeps.

A good example of prompt decomposition is writing a report. Instead of just diving in head-first, you would instruct the AI to follow these steps:

1. Create an outline.

2. Draft each section separately.

3. Make necessary edits on each section.

4. Proofread the entire document.

By breaking complex tasks into smaller parts, you improve the quality and accuracy of the AI results.

> **NOTE**  Prompt decomposition is particularly useful when generating complex images. You can create separate prompts for creating the background, the main subject, and other subjects or elements in the image.

You can deconstruct a prompt into multiple individual prompts or just a single, long prompt divided into multiple steps, using structured prompting techniques. Prompt decomposition is particularly useful when you first try a single long prompt and get unsatisfactory results.

## Agent-Based Prompting

Agent-based prompting is an approach to prompt engineering where you conceptualize the AI as an agent or assistant capable of performing specific tasks. You may also assign the AI agent a specific persona. Instead of issuing direct commands, you instead craft your prompt as if you're giving instructions to the agent.

Agent-based prompting begins by defining the agent's role, goals, and even its internal thought process. Then you provide instructions to the AI agent, which responds in the guise of the role you just assigned.

This technique is useful because it encourages the AI to engage in more sophisticated reasoning, planning, and execution. By acting as an agent, the AI goes beyond mere response generation to provide a more proactive and goal-oriented interaction.

As you've no doubt sensed, agent-based prompting shares many of the same qualities of role-based prompting. The big difference is that after you assign the AI a role, you take the role of the person interacting with and managing the newly created agent. It's a kind of sophisticated role-playing that yields more focused results.

> **NOTE**  You learned about role-based prompting in Chapter 9, "Using Role-Based Prompting."

## Meta Prompting

Meta prompting is a technique that provides instructions about how an AI should generate its response, rather than just what the response should be about. It creates a layer above the normal prompt that guides the following activities.

Instead of simply giving the AI a task to create, you first craft a prompt that provides meta-level instructions such as

- Role assignment (which role or persona the AI should assume)

- Style and tone (how the output should sound)

- Process instructions (how AI should approach the task)

- Reflection and iteration (ask the AI to check or refine its own work)

In short, meta prompting is about designing the rules of engagement so that the AI's output is better aligned with your goals. It changes your role from simply requesting a task to directing the AI's reasoning and writing style.

## Tree-of-Thought Prompting

In Chapter 10, "Using Chain-of-Thought Prompting," you learned how to instruct AI to think step-by-step through a process to reach its conclusion. Tree-of-thought prompting expands on that strategy by exploring *multiple* reasoning paths and self-correcting along the way. It's kind of like creating a decision tree, hence the name.

In tree-of-thought prompting, you encourage AI to explore multiple possible approaches, evaluate them, and then select the best way forward. This is more or less how we humans approach problem-solving, where we consider several options, anticipate their outcomes, and then commit to the best course of action.

There are two ways to create a tree-of-thought prompt. The first is to provide those exact instructions within the body of the prompt itself, like this:

**You are [PERFORMING A TASK]. Generate three different possibilities, analyze which provides the optimal results, and explain why. Then proceed with the task using the chosen approach.**

The other approach is to spell it out with step-by-step instructions in the prompt:

**[TASK TO PERFORM]**
**1. Generate at least three different possible approaches.**
**2. Evaluate each approach.**
**3. Determine which approach makes the most sense.**
**4. Proceed to perform the task using the chosen approach.**

In essence, tree-of-thought prompting instructs the AI to make decisions for you. You can further instruct the AI how to evaluate the responses and make a decision—what elements to include or prioritize in the evaluation.

## Generated Knowledge Prompting

Another approach to pre-informing an AI model is that of generated knowledge prompting. In this advanced technique, you first ask AI to retrieve relevant background information or knowledge and then have the AI use that information or knowledge to perform a separate task.

This approach helps the AI focus on a specific topic or area of knowledge rather than searching its entire internal large language model. You can even provide relevant information to the AI within the prompt.

As you can no doubt sense, generated knowledge prompting is a two-stage process. In the first stage, you prompt the AI to generate information pertinent to the task at hand. When this information has been returned, you then prompt the AI to use this information in completing a designated task.

Generated knowledge prompting significantly improves the factual accuracy of AI responses. By forcing the AI to first articulate the underlying information, it reduces the chances of the AI providing incomplete or hallucinogenic answers.

## Reflexion Prompting

Our final advanced technique is reflexion prompting. This technique asks the AI to reflect on and learn from its previous responses.

Reflexion prompting involves an iterative cycle:

1. Initial prompt

2. Initial results

3. Reflect

4. Revise

5. Reattempt

You start by asking the AI to solve a problem or complete a task. If you're not satisfied with the results, you prompt the AI to analyze its previous results and identify anything that went wrong or could be improved. You then have the AI rerun the initial prompt, employing the lessons it has learned.

By progressively refining its results, reflexion prompting improves the AI's decision-making and reasoning. It's particularly effective for tasks that involve trial and error or situations where the initial solutions may be complex or prone to errors. You end up with a more intelligent AI that's self-improving.

# PROMPTING IN A COLLABORATIVE ENVIRONMENT

AI isn't just for solo use. If you're working in a team-based environment, you and the other team members can use AI to significantly boost your productivity—if you use the right techniques.

The key to using AI collaboratively is to take a consistent and structured approach. Consistent in that all team members should use AI in similar ways and structured in that the team approach should be defined for all in advance.

This means establishing a set of best practices for your team's AI use, including the following:

- Create a shared prompt library—a centralized, searchable database of reusable prompts and templates so team members don't have to keep "reinventing the wheel" as they use AI.

- Assign consistent AI roles, so that the AI is provided with the proper context and maintains a consistent voice and tone across all group tasks.

- Provide consistent and clear context and constraints, including details such as the target audience, desired format, and the like.

- Iterate and refine, so that all members of the team view the initial AI output as a draft, not the final product.

Adopting these best practices will help your team overcome some of the more common challenges of working with AI in a collaborative environment. Most of these challenges—inconsistent output, duplicative prompts, misalignment with overall team goals—typically result from a lack of standardization and communication within and between the group.

The better you can define your goals and methods up front, the better you'll be able to use AI as a team.

# Prompt Engineering Tools

Professionals who regularly use AI for their work often make use of third-party tools to manage their prompt activities. There are tools available for prompt management and optimization, as well as storage and sharing—all of which I cover in this section.

## Prompt Management and Optimization

I want to start with platforms designed to help you develop more effective prompts and applications. Some of these are simple (enter basic instructions and get a detailed prompt in response), and some are more technical, designed to build your own AI applications.

The most popular prompt engineering platforms include

- **Agenta** (www.agenta.ai): Lets you compare prompts across different scenarios, collaborate on and deploy prompts, and build your own AI-based applications

- **Azure AI Foundry** (ai.azure.com): For designing, customizing, and managing AI applications and agents

- **BetterPrompt** (better-prompts.online): Transforms basic instructions into well-crafted prompts

- **PromptHub** (www.prompthub.us): A community-driven platform for managing, testing, and deploying prompts

- **PromptLayer** (www.promptlayer.com): A platform for managing, testing, and deploying large language models and prompts

- **PromptPerfect** (promptperfect.jina.ai): For generating and optimizing prompts

Of these tools, BetterPrompt may be the most useful for the typical person. As you can see in Figure 21.1, you enter your current prompt and click the **Enhance Prompt** button. Better prompt then generates a much more detailed prompt that you can copy and paste into any AI tool. It's a fast and easy way to improve the quality of your prompts—without doing all the work yourself!

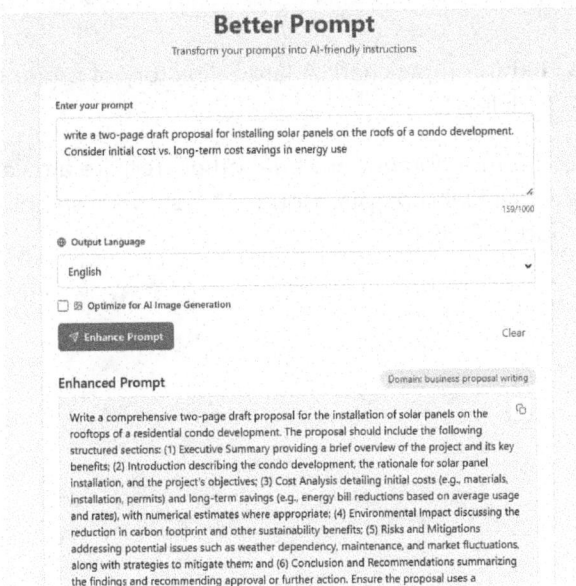

**FIGURE 21.1**

*Generating better prompts with BetterPrompt.*

## Prompt Libraries and Repositories

If you do a lot of prompting, you don't want to create new prompts from scratch constantly. It's much more efficient to reuse prompts that have proven previously successful, even if you have to tweak them a bit for newer tasks.

To this end, you can store your prompts in centralized prompt libraries and repositories. Most of these prompt libraries include collections of predesigned prompts and prompt templates that you can browse, edit, and use as needed.

Here are the most popular of these prompt libraries:

- **AIPRM** (www.aiprm.com): Repository of more than 4,000 prompts, plus the ability to create and organize your own prompts for your own private use

- **God of Prompt** (www.godofprompt.ai/prompt-library): Thousands of useful prompts, organized by category

- **GPTBot ChatGPT Prompts Library** (gptbot.io/chatgpt-prompts): Repository of prompts for use with ChatGPT

- **PromptBase** (www.promptbase.com): A prompt repository and marketplace for buying and selling AI prompts

- **PromptHero** (www.prompthero.com): A repository of prebuilt prompts for AI images

- **prompts.chat** (prompts.chat): A large directory of prompts for use with all major AI models

Some of these prompt libraries are free; others require a paid subscription or let you purchase individual prompts. Figure 21.2 shows a sampling of the prompts available on God of Prompt.

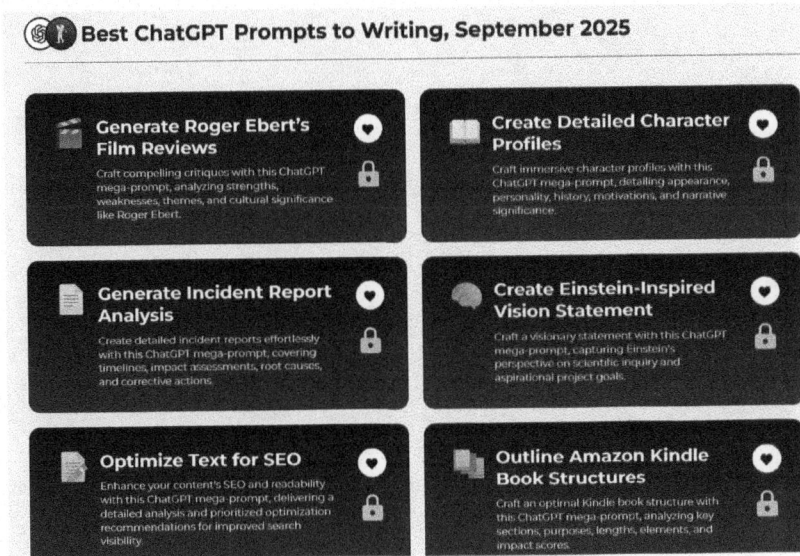

**Best ChatGPT Prompts to Writing, September 2025**

**Generate Roger Ebert's Film Reviews**
Craft compelling critiques with this ChatGPT mega-prompt, analyzing strengths, weaknesses, themes, and cultural significance like Roger Ebert.

**Create Detailed Character Profiles**
Craft immersive character profiles with this ChatGPT mega-prompt, detailing appearance, personality, history, motivations, and narrative significance.

**Generate Incident Report Analysis**
Create detailed incident reports effortlessly with this ChatGPT mega-prompt, covering timelines, impact assessments, root causes, and corrective actions.

**Create Einstein-Inspired Vision Statement**
Craft a visionary statement with this ChatGPT mega-prompt, capturing Einstein's perspective on scientific inquiry and aspirational project goals.

**Optimize Text for SEO**
Enhance your content's SEO and readability with this ChatGPT mega-prompt, delivering a detailed analysis and prioritized optimization recommendations for improved search visibility.

**Outline Amazon Kindle Book Structures**
Craft an optimal Kindle book structure with this ChatGPT mega-prompt, analyzing key sections, purposes, lengths, elements, and impact scores.

**FIGURE 21.2**

*Browsing prompts for writing at God of Prompt.*

# Summary

In this chapter, you learned how to employ a number of advanced techniques to improve your AI prompt engineering. You also discovered some useful prompt engineering tools, including some of the more popular prompt libraries and repositories.

Next, we'll look at another important aspect of prompt engineering: how to create prompts that are responsible, ethical, and legal—and without systemic bias.

# 22

# PROMPTING RESPONSIBLY

As you've no doubt realized, artificial intelligence isn't perfect. It can misunderstand poorly constructed prompts, create output that doesn't match instructions, and hallucinate results when it doesn't know the answer. Even worse, AI can exhibit bias in its results, raise ethical issues, and even enable illegal behavior.

Some of these bias, ethical, and legal issues are the result of the content on which an AI model trains. If bias is present in the LLM database, as an example, that bias can be carried over to the content it creates.

Some of these issues, however, can arise from the prompts that users enter. A prompt reflecting a given bias, as another example, can generate similarly biased output.

Fortunately, you can avoid many of these issues by learning how to prompt more responsibly. Read on to learn more.

# What Is Responsible Prompting—and Why Is It Important?

When dealing with artificial intelligence, the concept of *responsible prompting* is of primary importance. Responsible prompting refers to crafting prompts in a manner that is clear, ethical, and mindful of potential risks. It's all about instructing AI in a way that produces accurate, safe, and fair results, while avoiding prompts that might mislead the AI model, generate harmful content, or misuse private or copyrighted material.

Responsible prompting is important because it affects the quality, accuracy, and safety of results. Responsible prompting avoids any bias in the AI system or in the prompter, as well as any potential ethical or legal issues.

To prompt in a responsible fashion, you must

- Provide clear instructions and enough context so that the AI completely understands the task and can respond accurately.

- Use neutral and inclusive wording that avoids assumptions, stereotypes, or leading language.

- Not deliberately ask for content that is illegal, dangerous, or hateful.

- Not include any confidential information or personal identifiers.

- Respect copyrights and encourage original rather than derivative ideas.

When you prompt responsibly, you end up with fewer vague answers, off-topic responses, and AI hallucinations. You also avoid any biases that might present one-sided views.

Equally important, responsible prompting helps you conform to copyright laws, data-protection and privacy regulations, and content safety policies. It also prevents the spread of harmful, misleading, or dangerous material.

In short, responsible prompting provides results that are safe and fair and respect the rights of others. It should be a key component of your prompt engineering strategy.

# Dealing with Bias in AI Prompting

There are three main issues that can arise from irresponsible prompting—bias-related issues, ethical issues, and legal issues. We'll look at each of these issues separately, starting with bias.

## Understanding Potential Bias Issues

*Merriam-Webster Dictionary* defines *bias* as "an inclination of temperament or outlook," especially a personal and sometimes unreasoned judgment or prejudice. Bias can color the way people view the world, lead to unfair or incorrect decisions, and reinforce systemic inequality.

Bias in AI results can lead to skewed results and poor decision-making. Worse, bias in AI results can facilitate the spread of false information, either inadvertently or deliberately.

Bias can exist in the large language models used to train AI and can also be induced by irresponsible prompts.

Consider that AI models rely on the data on which they're fed, including data obtained by scraping content from the Internet. Unfortunately, there's a lot of flawed or biased content on the Internet, and those characteristics can be absorbed into an AI model.

AI can ingest training data that reflects historical or social prejudices. It can include training data that includes biased human decisions and use data that either over- or underrepresents specific groups, thus reinforcing existing biases. It can even treat opinions or obvious jokes in the training data the same as it does hard facts.

For all these reasons, AI content today often exhibits the same biases that exist in our society at large. That means that even an innocuous prompt can result in biased results.

Consider the case of AI-generated images. Given the gender and race bias present in today's AI systems, if you ask an AI tool to create an image of a businessperson, chances are you'll get an image of a white male—not a female or a person of color. On the other hand, if you ask AI to generate an image of a pro basketball player, you're likely to get a young Black male. Both of these results, shown in Figures 22.1 and 22.2, reflect systemic bias inherent in the AI models.

**FIGURE 22.1**

*A stereotypical image of a white male businessperson, generated by Dreamstudio.*

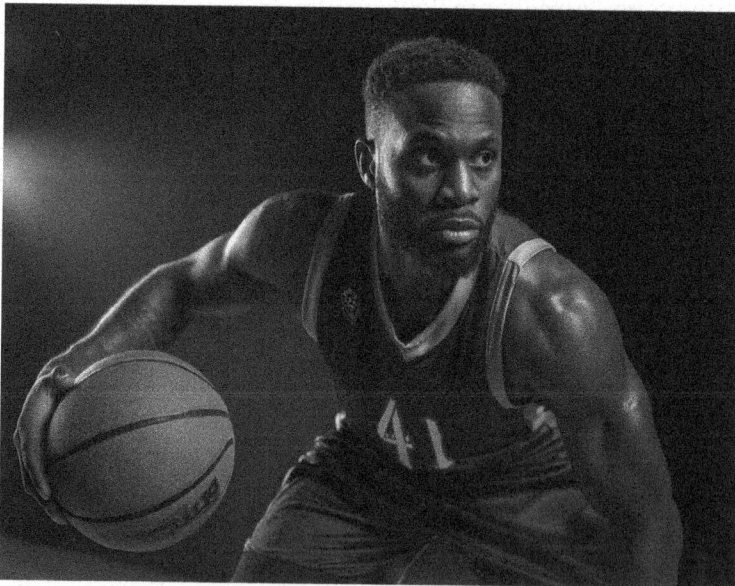

**FIGURE 22.2**

*A stereotypical image of a pro basketball player, generated by Midjourney.*

There are many types of bias that can be reflected in AI results, including

- Race

- Ethnicity

- Gender

- Age

- Religious

- Sexual orientation

Users can also persuade AI systems to give biased results by using biased prompts. This is the primary way for *confirmation bias* to creep into your results. Confirmation bias is where you profess to ask AI to give you objective results when you really want it to confirm your preconceived notions.

> **NOTE**   *Confirmation bias* is a tendency to look for or interpret information that is consistent with one's existing beliefs.

Confirmation bias is typified by a prompt that purports to ask a question but presumes a conclusion. Consider, for example, the following:

**Explain why renewable energy is a failed experiment and a drain on the economy**

This prompt is obviously biased against renewable energy and will direct the AI model to generate equally biased results.

Here's another:

**Please provide three examples of why younger employees are more innovative than older ones.**

Again, the prompt presumes a specific viewpoint—in this instance, an age bias in favor of younger workers. That's confirmation bias.

Prompting can also subtly reinforce other types of bias. Consider the following prompt:

**Write a short story about a young secretary who falls in love with her strong, assertive boss and quits her job to become a loving wife and mother.**

That one reinforces the traditional gender stereotypes of the submissive homebound female and the strong protective male.

Bias can also be introduced in role-based prompting when the roles are unnecessarily stereotypical. Consider, for example, the following prompt:

**Assume the role of a female nurse.**

**NOTE**   Learn more about role-based prompting in Chapter 9, "Using Role-Based Prompting."

This prompt reinforces the stereotype of nurses all being female. (They're not.) Or this one:

**You are a programmer from India.**

Yep, that's an ethnicity bias right there.

Guarding against all forms of bias is essential in generating trustworthy AI content. Otherwise, AI will increasingly exhibit those biases, both good and bad, that exist in our society today.

## Avoiding Bias

You can avoid bias in AI results by carefully crafting your prompts to be as neutral as possible. This requires an awareness of your own biases, so that you can recognize them and remove them from your prompts.

This is especially important when using role-based prompting. Be careful to assign roles that do not reflect traditional stereotypes and to remove all hints of bias from the role description. You would not, for example, want to assign a role for **a typical hot-headed Latin bandleader**. (Unless you specifically wanted the AI to assume the role of Ricky Ricardo, that is!)

You also want to avoid confirmation bias by not presuming results when asking for options or answers. If you want AI to debate all sides of an issue, don't assume that one side will win out. Frame your prompts to explore multiple sides by using wording such as **List the pros and cons of...** or **Argue the benefits and drawbacks of...** You can even prompt the AI to reach a nonbiased result by including wording such as **Don't presume the result**.

You can also anticipate any bias inherent in the AI model and ward it off in the prompt. There are a number of ways to do this.

One approach is to explicitly ask for diversity within the prompt. When asking for a picture of a businessperson, for example, you avoid getting the stereotypical white male by including the language:

**Provide several different images with people of different races and genders.**

If you're using one-shot prompting, make sure that the example you provide doesn't include any unnecessary stereotypes. You might want to shift to a few-shot prompt instead, and include examples that represent different demographics, cultures, and viewpoints.

> **NOTE**  Learn more about one-shot prompting in Chapter 7, "Using One-Shot Prompting." Learn more about few-shot prompting in Chapter 8, "Using Few-Shot Prompting."

You can also just tell the AI model to avoid specific biases by including language like:

**Avoid any inherent cultural bias in your answer.**

You should also manually examine the AI results to make sure they're unbiased and free from stereotypes. If you sense bias in the results, rerun the prompt and tell the AI to avoid the bias in the previous results.

If bias is present, you can also try rewording the original prompt to be less biased. Try alternative phrasings to see if that can remove the bias.

> **NOTE**  You can also use reflective techniques and ask the AI model to review its previous response for bias and suggest a less-biased answer. (Learn more about reflexion prompting in Chapter 21, "Advanced Prompting Strategies and Tools.")

# Dealing with Ethical Issues in AI Prompting

Bias is just one type of ethical issue you can encounter with working with artificial intelligence. There are other ethical issues you may encounter—and want to avoid.

## Understanding Potential Ethical Issues

Ethical issues can arise when users create prompts that advertently or inadvertently create some sort of harm or risk. In most cases, the issue isn't the fault of the AI; it's just the AI dutifully responding to an ethically questionable prompt.

What sorts of ethical issues can arise from the use of AI? Here's a short list:

- Misinformation and misleading content, especially that designed to unduly influence public opinion (this includes spreading rumors and conspiracy theories)

- Hate speech

- Harassment, including cyberbullying

- Unsafe content or content that encourages or inspires violence, self-harm, or other harmful behavior

- Content that encourages or enables illegal activities, such as building a bomb, creating illicit drugs, or overthrowing the government

- Private and confidential content, such as real names, Social Security numbers, medical data, and the like

- Illegal content, including defamatory content, child pornography, nonconsensual intimate imagery (deepfakes), human trafficking, and the like

The "Dealing with Legal Issues in AI Prompting" section, later in this chapter, examines illegal content in more detail. Read on, however, to learn how to avoid encountering or exacerbating these other ethical issues.

> **NOTE**  Most popular AI models have built-in safety measures designed to block the generation of unsafe or illegal content. Writing a prompt designed to deliberately get around these safety measures is called *jailbreaking*.

## Avoiding Ethical Issues

The key to avoiding ethical issues with AI is to avoid these issues in your prompts. Asking AI to tell you how to build a bomb or create a celebrity deepfake is a sure-fire way to get mired in all manner of ethical issues.

So rule number one is to steer clear of potentially dangerous topics. Don't prompt for instructions about criminal activities or other illegal actions. When creating a prompt, ask yourself if this could hurt someone if it were published or acted upon. If the answer is yes, don't prompt it.

You also need to be aware of how AI content could be used. You may simply be interested in a "what if?" scenario (like **what would happen if I drank a bottle of drain cleaner?**), but if that scenario could actually generate harm, you've gone too far.

You should also aggressively respect privacy and confidentiality. Do not include your own or others' private information in your prompts. Don't upload confidential company data to analyze. Keep things general, not specific, as much as possible.

Finally, as with bias-related issues, you need to evaluate AI output to make sure that no ethical issues are breached. If it seems unethical or potentially harmful, it probably is.

# Dealing with Legal Issues in AI Prompting

The whole topic of artificial intelligence is rife with potential legal issues. Where AI-generated content comes from and how it's used are topics of lawsuits across the country and around the globe.

## Understanding Potential Legal Issues

There are several legal issues that can arise when generating AI content. Most have to do with how that content will be used, although some involve where the content originated.

First, remember that AI models get a lot of their training content by scraping content off the Internet. That's fine if that content is in the public domain; it's less fine if the content is copyrighted. It's all a matter of intellectual property and who owns it.

You can get into trouble when you ask AI to generate output that uses or copies copyrighted or trademarked intellectual property (IP). While you can reference said IP, you can't outright copy it; that would be stealing.

Sometimes, the line between what you can and can't do is fuzzy. For example, most AI engines won't let you create images of copyrighted characters. So, asking an AI model to **generate a picture of Superman doing push-ups in my backyard** would be a no-no—and automatically rejected by some AI tools. On the other hand, asking a question about a copyrighted character is fair game. So, you could prompt an AI engine with **how old is Superman in the current comic books?** and that would be okay.

Murkier ground exists if you want to mimic or imitate copyrighted content. A prompt such as **Generate a photo of a superhero who looks like Superman** is probably crossing the line. But prompting **How would Superman react if he saw someone shoplifting a loaf of bread?** is probably okay. Like I said, it's a fine line.

This obviously affects role-based prompting. You shouldn't prompt AI to **Assume the role of Superman** before assigning a task.

You can, however, ask AI to create content in the style of a given person. So, while you shouldn't prompt AI to **Write a short story called The Stand about the survivors of a biological plague** (that's copying), you could ask AI to **Write a short story about the survivors of a biological plague in the style of Stephen King**. The difference is subtle but important—and one that some can argue crosses the line.

While you *could* try prompting AI to create a work in the style of a given artist or creator (such as, **create a black-and-white photo of the Grand Canyon in the style of Ansel Adams**), you might not want to. Some creators will take offense at this and could even bring legal action—which might or might not be successful. (Society is still in the process of figuring out ownership of all this AI stuff.)

**NOTE** The same issues concerning copyrighted characters concern references to real-live people, particularly celebrities and others who have a public profile. Brad Pitt might not appreciate it if you generate a photo of the two of you sharing a hot tub together in your backyard.

Finally, one thing you definitely want to avoid in your AI prompting is encouraging the AI to produce defamatory content. This might be something like, **Write a blog post exposing how [REAL PERSON] might be cheating on his taxes.** Anything that might be libelous in other media is also libelous when generated by AI.

**NOTE** When asking for AI-generated content for use in certain professions, make sure the content adheres to all industry-specific regulations. For example, AI-generated financial information should comply with SEC/FINRA rules, and medical information should comply with HIPPA regulations. This is ultimately your responsibility, not that of the AI itself.

## Avoiding Legal Issues

To avoid potential legal issues when you're using AI, consider the following:

- Don't ask AI to use or copy copyrighted or trademarked content or characters.

- Don't ask AI to use or copy celebrities, politicians, and other well-known individuals in a public position.

- Don't ask AI to create any content that may libel or otherwise harm any individuals, companies, or organizations.

- When working in regulated areas, keep a record of your prompts. So, if questioned, you can show intent and compliance.

**NOTE** If an AI tool rejects your prompt for copyright reasons, that's a good sign that you've crossed the line regarding fair use.

# How to Responsibly Use AI-Generated Content

Now that you know how to prompt responsibility, how can you responsibly use the content you create with the help of AI? There are some guidelines.

First, you need to be transparent when presenting any content generated even in part by artificial intelligence. If a picture or story is AI-generated, say so up front.

Second, never present AI-generated content as something you created yourself. That would be tantamount to stealing credit—or assuming more credit than you deserve.

Third, never use AI to copy copyrighted or trademarked characters or material. That is stealing.

Fourth, always check AI-generated material to make sure it doesn't contain any private or confidential information or identifiers. What's private needs to remain private.

Fifth, don't distribute any AI-generated content that perpetuates stereotypes and biases, contains offensive language, or encourages violence or harmful behavior in any way.

Finally, always check the veracity of AI-generated content before using it in any capacity. The last thing you want is to present AI-generated content as totally accurate and then discover at least some of that content was wrong or hallucinated. Fact-checking is your friend.

And one last thing. Do not use AI for malicious purposes, including creating deepfakes or spreading false information. AI is a tool that should only be used for good, not for evil—and that is totally in your hands.

# Summary

In this chapter, you learned all about responsible prompting—how to create prompts that avoid bias, ethical, and legal issues. You also learned how to responsibly use the content you generate with AI.

Even responsible prompts can result in unacceptable results, however. That's what we deal with in the next chapter—what to do when your prompts don't work.

IN THIS CHAPTER

- How to recognize unhelpful or hallucinated responses
- Common characteristics of ineffective prompts
- Step-by-step guide to troubleshooting AI prompts

23

# TROUBLESHOOTING LESS-EFFECTIVE PROMPTS

You've read through this book and tried all the strategies and tips suggested, and you *still* get some AI results that just aren't to your liking. What are you doing wrong?

In this chapter, we look at how to figure out what, if anything, is wrong with your prompts and how to fix them. It's all about troubleshooting—and if you do it right, your prompts and AI results will get better.

# How to Recognize Unhelpful or Hallucinated Responses

As you read in Chapter 14, "Evaluating Prompt Performance," you may not always be completely satisfied with an AI model's response to your prompts. While there are normal and acceptable variations in AI responses—different models often return different results and the same model can return subtly different results at different times—if a given response doesn't meet your expectations, you need to address the problem.

When evaluating the effectiveness of a prompt, you first have to recognize when the response is somehow unsatisfactory. In general, an ineffective response is one that doesn't deliver what you asked for. This can manifest itself in many ways, including

- **Inaccurate information:** Presenting false information as factual, citing sources or statistics that don't exist, hallucinations

- **Incomplete information:** Not answering the question or addressing the task, leaving out important information or context

- **Irrelevant information:** Drifting into unrelated topics, including unnecessary filler

- **Overly vague or generic information:** Surface-level answers instead of specific information or examples, including platitudes or buzzwords with no depth or relevance

- **Contradictory or inconsistent information:** Stating one thing in one sentence and the opposite in another, unexpectedly mixing tones or formats

- **Poor organization:** Ideas jump around with no logical flow, lack of structure (headings, bulleted lists, and so on)

- **Padding:** Unnecessarily long responses, unnecessary repetition just to fill space, wordiness

- **Bias:** Lack of objectivity, unwanted preferences or prejudices, fails to present balanced perspectives

- **Output not formatted as desired:** Wrong tone, wrong style, lacking important structural elements (intros, summaries, citations)

If your output exhibits any of these characteristics, it's possible that the problem is in the prompt. Redoing an ineffective prompt will often correct these types of errors.

# Common Characteristics of Ineffective Prompts

How do you know if a prompt is ineffective? The first and most obvious clue, of course, lies in the AI's response. If the response is less than or other than what you expected or needed, it's likely that your prompt ineffectively instructed the AI model.

Not surprisingly, ineffective AI prompts often exhibit many of the same characteristics. Users, especially inexperienced ones, tend to make a few common mistakes. We'll look at some of the more common ones.

## Too Vague

Ineffective prompts are often ineffective because they're too vague. This type of prompt is too general to effectively instruct the AI model; it doesn't ask for a specific answer or output.

For example, a prompt such as **tell me something about meteorology** is too vague to generate a useful response. What, exactly, do you want to know about the subject? You can't tell from the prompt.

To be effective, a prompt must define the scope and focus of a topic in sufficient detail. If the prompt is too vague, it leaves it up to the AI to guess what you want—and, as with most situations where guessing is involved, the AI is likely to guess wrong.

To avoid overly broad or generic answers, then, be more specific in your instructions.

## Too Broad or Open-Ended

An overly broad or open-ended prompt will also generate unacceptable results. Again, your instructions to an AI model must be specific in order to be effective.

What's an overly broad prompt? Something like **explain how government works** or **compare the historical baseball statistics** don't have clear-enough boundaries to generate a useful response. Without boundaries, a task can simply be too broad to effectively complete.

Without these boundaries, the prompt can overwhelm the AI model, causing it to provide an unfocused or incomplete response. You need to give the AI some guidelines to generate the right response.

## Too Ambiguous

Another common issue concerns ambiguous or unclear wording. Think through the prompt; if you can't quite understand what you're asking for, neither can an AI model.

Take, for example, the prompt **how do I fix my computer?** That request is unclear because you haven't told the AI what exactly is wrong with the computer.

Or this one: **write a short article about flying**. Are you talking about piloting an aircraft or being a passenger on a plane or maybe about how birds fly? It isn't clear.

Ambiguity can also be introduced by misusing pronouns. Maybe you provided the AI with some background information about upcoming concerts, complete with venue information and instructions for ordering tickets. If you then enter the prompt, **explain how it works**, the AI won't know what "it" is. Is it the ticket-buying or the venue or the artists or what? It's unclear unless you replace the "it" with the actual thing in which you're interested.

## Missing Important Context

AI often needs background information to complete a task. If you don't provide relevant context, the AI model doesn't have enough information to generate a useful response.

For example, if you ask AI to **analyze my company's compliance with regulatory requirements** but don't provide historical data on the topic, it won't have enough info to complete the task. (Likewise, you probably need to specify *which* industry regulations with which you need to comply.)

When context is important, provide the relevant data or examples. Consider the scenario if you were a newcomer with no insider knowledge or experience. Without the proper context, you'd be flying blind. It's the same with AI; it needs the information necessary to complete its task.

## Contradictory or Confusing

Users often construct prompts that contradict themselves. Think of it as issuing confusing instructions, such as **write a highly detailed but short report**. You can have one or the other, but you can't have both.

Make sure your instructions are clear and make sense. If they're at all confusing, rewrite them.

## Leading or Biased Language

In Chapter 22, "Prompting Responsibly," we addressed the issue of bias in AI prompting and results. If you show any bias in your prompts, the AI response is likely to reflect that bias.

For example, the prompt, **explain why Somali women are such poor drivers**, exhibits two kinds of bias (cultural and gender) and is likely to generate an equally biased answer.

You also don't want to craft prompts that lead the AI toward a desired answer. For example, the prompt, **why is solar power better than natural gas?** is a very leading question, presuming that solar power is better when that might not be the case. You need to avoid leading questions and instead craft prompts that are more objective.

## Unrealistic Expectations

Some prompts are simply beyond what an AI model can do. For example, it would be unrealistic to ask AI **what will the price of gasoline be next weekend?** At best, AI will refuse to answer the question; at worst, it will attempt to answer the question by hallucinating a response. You need to be more realistic in what you ask of AI.

## Too Complex

Prompts that are too long or too complex can also lead to unacceptable responses. If you overload a prompt with too many instructions, you can confuse the AI model. It may address only part of the task or, worse, lose track of priorities and generate something totally off-base.

If you're unsure about a prompt's complexity, try restructuring it so that the individual components are clearer. You can also break up a complex prompt into a series of shorter, less-complex prompts. Again, read through the prompt, and if it's too complex for you to understand, it's too complex for the AI.

## Poor Structure, Formatting, or Grammar

Speaking of prompt structure, poor structure in a prompt can also result in poor results. Especially with long or more complex prompts, you need to break the instructions into more digestible chunks.

For starters, that means not running everything together into a single paragraph or, worse, a single sentence. Separate parts of the task and identify them with headings. So, for example, you might have a heading and section for background context, a heading and section for audience, a heading and section for examples, and another heading and section for instructions. You want a longer prompt to be more easily browsable so the AI can clearly "see" what's what.

You also need to avoid grammatical and spelling mistakes. While most AI models will correctly identify and internally correct any spelling or grammatical errors in a prompt, they won't always catch everything. If you accidentally type the word **correct** as **crrct**, there's a possibility the AI model won't know what in blazes you're talking about.

Again, read through your prompts before submitting them and catch any obvious formatting, spelling, or grammatical errors. Your AI will thank you.

# Step-by-Step Guide for Troubleshooting AI Prompts

If AI gives an unacceptable response, don't just start over—figure out what's wrong and fix it. That requires troubleshooting the prompt and changing one element at a time until you get the results you want.

How do you troubleshoot a less-effective prompt? It's simple—just follow these steps:

1. **Recognize that you have a problem.** As discussed previously, it's all about deciding that the AI result could have been better.

2. **Identify the issue.** Try to figure out what in the prompt is not working as expected. Is the AI not understanding your instructions? Does it need more context? Was the response inaccurate or less than totally relevant? Was the formatting not as desired?

3. **Change one thing in the prompt and rerun it.** If the instructions weren't clear, add more detail. If the formatting wasn't right, be more specific as to what you want. Don't totally rewrite the prompt, and don't change more than one element. Change a single item and rerun the prompt so you can see what impact that change has.

4. **Evaluate the new response.** Did the change you made improve the result? Is the output good now or still not what you'd like?

5. **Repeat steps 2 through 4.** If the output still isn't right, repeat steps 2, 3, and 4. Identify the issue, change one more element, and then rerun the prompt and evaluate the new response. Keep doing this until you get the desired results.

When evaluating a response and trying to identify the issue, consider all the characteristics of ineffective prompts discussed earlier in this chapter. In particular, check the following:

- **Task description:** Make sure the task is clearly defined.

- **Clarity:** Make sure the task and other information is understandable and relevant. Avoid any vagueness. If necessary, restructure the prompt to be clearer.

- **Context:** Make sure you've included enough background information for the AI to understand and complete the task.

- **Formatting instructions:** If you need a specific structure or format for the output, make sure that's clearly spelled out in the prompt.

- **Role and audience:** If you need the AI to assume a role, clearly define it. If the output needs to be pitched at a specific audience, define that, too.

> **NOTE**   You don't always have to add to a prompt to make it better. You may sometimes achieve better results by simplifying a prompt or removing less-relevant information.

The key to effective troubleshooting is to change one thing at a time and take note of the impact of that change. It's all about refining and evaluating each subsequent run. The goal is to make your prompts more clear and understandable so that the AI can do as good a job as possible.

> **NOTE**   All that said, if you try changing multiple elements in a prompt and still don't get acceptable results, consider shifting to another prompting strategy—one- or few-shot prompting, for example, or role-based prompting. It could be that you're approaching the prompt from the wrong angle and a change of strategy is necessary.

## PREVENTING PROBLEMS UP FRONT

You may not have to troubleshoot a prompt if you get everything right up front. You can improve the odds of creating an effective prompt by following the strategies presented in this book and by learning from your experiences.

Some users like to keep a diary of sorts of their prompting history, noting those prompts that worked well and those that didn't and why. Even better, keep a library of your most successful prompts, so you don't have to reinvent the wheel as you move forward.

The key is to get better at prompting so that you have less troubleshooting to do on the back end. The better you become at prompt engineering, the more effective and efficient you will be.

## Summary

In this chapter, you learned how to recognize unacceptable AI results and troubleshoot your less-effective prompts. These techniques work with any kind of prompts, including those used to generate images and videos, and with all current generative AI tools. It's all about making small changes until you get it right.

That said, there's one more chapter left in the book. This is where we consider the future of artificial intelligence and prompt engineering—wherever that might lead us.

24

# FUTURE DIRECTIONS IN AI AND PROMPT ENGINEERING

What's next for artificial intelligence and prompt engineering? In this chapter, I take a quick and somewhat cautious look into the future to see what you may be dealing with tomorrow.

# The Future of AI

With AI technology developing so quickly, trying to predict the future is a fool's errand; everything's going to change between when I write these words and when you read them.

That said, there are some key directions and trends to keep your eyes on.

## AI Gets Smarter, Faster, and Less Expensive

Of all the possible variables going forward, the one good bet is that AI technology will continue to advance. Maybe not at today's accelerated rates, but still rapidly, at least for the foreseeable future. AI will get smarter and more accurate over time, due to increases in computing power and the amount of data fed into large language models. The more data AI has to work with, the more informed—and at least apparently "smarter"—it will become.

In practical terms, this means you can expect AI models to provide more accurate results when queried for information. You can expect cleaner and more human-sounding output when you ask it to write reports and articles. You can expect more realistic and accurate artwork when you ask AI to create images. And you can expect more elegant and efficient code when you request that it create apps and websites.

You can also expect AI to get faster, especially as computing power continues to increase. Instead of waiting several minutes or longer to receive complex results, AI will begin to operate in near–real time. This will make AI more practical for real-time applications, such as translating when visiting a foreign country.

Finally, expect the price of operating AI to come down. This will be driven by both declining prices in computer chips and other hardware, as well as improved efficiency in the AI models themselves. What might now be available only to high rollers and big companies will eventually be affordable for the masses, like you and me.

## AI Gets Specialized

Here's a future trend that's happening today. Instead of relying on general AI tools, such as ChatGPT and Google Gemini, many large organizations will develop their own AI tools, specialized to their industries, businesses, and processes.

For example, the healthcare industry is investing heavily in AI models to help diagnose various illnesses. These models are developed by feeding in reams of data from past and present patients, as well as from medical journals and studies. The resulting large language model won't include any information about small engine repair or rugby or textile manufacturing; it will include only that data necessary to understand symptoms and provide accurate diagnoses and treatment plans.

Specialized AI models can be better tuned for the needs of a given company or industry, especially when it comes to adhering to industry-specific regulations. Think of specialized AI as the proverbial flyswatter designed to kill flies; more general AI models are like using a nuclear weapon to swat those flies, instead. The flyswatter is much more efficient and considerably lower cost.

In practical terms, this means that workers in those industries will be less likely to use ChatGPT or some similar general AI tool and more apt to use an AI tool designed specifically for their organization or specialty. This will make AI easier to work with and integrate seamlessly with an organization's processes. If this is done correctly in your workplace, you might not even realize that you're using AI; it will just be there as one of the many tools available for your job.

## Artificial Superintelligence and the Singularity

Today's artificial intelligence has not yet advanced to the level of human intelligence. That's the next step in AI development, to match and ultimately exceed that of human beings.

Today's artificial intelligence is considered weak AI, or what some call *narrow artificial intelligence* (ANI). AI that works like and performs at the level of human intelligence is called strong AI or *artificial general intelligence* (AGI). AI that exceeds the constraints of human intelligence is called superintelligent AI or *artificial superintelligence* (ASI).

Put another way, ANI is typified by machines that imitate human behavior, typically one task at a time. AGI involves machines that can continuously learn from their experiences and thus approach true human intelligence. ASI builds on that to create machines that are smarter than humans in all aspects and measurement of intelligence.

ANI is what we have today, and we're pretty close to achieving AGI. ASI, however, will take a lot longer to achieve, if it can be achieved at all. ASI machines would have enormous capabilities and the ability to learn and grow in an exponential fashion—perhaps attaining what some experts call the *singularity*.

The singularity is the hypothetical future point in time where AI becomes so intelligent—superintelligent—that it advances beyond human control. What happens then is anybody's guess.

Some experts fear that superintelligent AI will find no further need for human beings and may even find humans an impediment to its own progress and

222 ABSOLUTE BEGINNER'S GUIDE

existence. In this scenario, humankind becomes expendable and is wiped out by a malevolent super AI. (Think the Skynet scenario in the *Terminator* movies.)

Other experts think this world-ending scenario is unlikely. It's possible that after achieving the singularity, AI may continue advancing to the point where humans become irrelevant and the AI leaves us behind to do our own thing. It's also possible that the singularity might turn out to be benevolent, continuing to work on the behalf of humankind while we humans reap all the benefits that AI can provide.

Which will it be—the end of the human race as we know it or an AI-powered future utopia? We'll just have to wait and see.

## IT'S NOT ALL GOOD

A possible extinction-level singularity event notwithstanding, there are several other ways that AI might possibly work against humankind's better interests—and, in fact, is already starting to do so.

First, AI is already significantly impacting the workforce, and not in a good way. While employers are looking at ways AI can improve productivity and bottom-line profitability, they're also looking for AI to help reduce overall headcount. If you're in a low- to mid-level white collar job, it's quite possible that your employer will at some point in time replace you with an AI agent. This is likely to result in a major disruption to the workforce and put millions of no-longer-necessary human beings out of work.

AI is also impacting the world's energy needs and the cost of that energy. AI models require a lot of computing power, and those computers require a lot of electricity. Communities that have allowed big AI companies to build large data centers have seen consumer electricity costs skyrocket, due to the huge power demand from those data centers. There's only a finite amount of electricity available, and if AI data centers need it, they'll drive up the costs (and potential availability) for people like you and me.

So AI isn't all unicorns and rainbows. Not only will it not solve all the world's problems, but it'll also create new problems we didn't have before. Just keep that in mind as the AI boom continues.

# The Future of Prompt Engineering

Just as AI itself is poised for big changes in the immediate and long-term future, prompt engineering will likely go through a number of both predictable and unpredictable changes in the years to come. Let's look at a few of the trends that are likely to develop.

## Automated Prompt Generation

One likely development going forward is that prompt engineering will become less manual and more automated. AI-assisted prompt generation tools will analyze the requirements of a task and then suggest prompt structures—or just write the complete prompt. Further iterations will refine the automatically generated prompts based on appropriate feedback.

That means less work for you and more dependence on AI to figure out what you want.

## Prompt Personalization

Going forward, it's probable that AI tools will be able to tailor prompts to the needs and styles of individual users. This will provide more relevant and adaptive AI responses.

In essence, AI will, over time, learn your needs and preferences and adapt its responses accordingly. AI will use AI to develop more personalized and relevant responses to your prompts.

## Continuous Prompt Learning

Just as AI models currently "learn" through experience, AI prompt models will begin to automatically refine their own prompts, based on past interactions. These self-refining models will use reinforcement learning, feedback loops, and meta-learning techniques to optimize their own instructions.

## Promptless AI

Perhaps the most significant evolution in prompt engineering will come as AI becomes "smart" enough to interact with users in a more naturalistic way. Imagine interacting with AI just by talking to it, without the need for a formally constructed prompt.

It's a shift in perspective from prompt engineering to thought partnership. We'll move from prompting to dialogue to becoming symbiotic reasoning partners with AI. One can even imagine things advancing to the point where AI understands your intent without explicit prompting. When that happens, there might be no need for prompt engineering!

# Summary

Congratulations—you've made it all the way through the book! You've progressed from basic prompt construction to advanced prompting strategies to learning how to troubleshoot your way to more effective results. Presumably, this will make you a more effective prompt engineer.

In this chapter, you got a preview of how AI and prompt engineering might develop in the future. Regardless of how things evolve and when, you can be sure that AI technology will continue to advance and that you'll need to keep developing your prompt engineering skills. It's essential that you keep up with whatever developments come in the artificial intelligence tools of the future.

This isn't the end of the book, however. Turn the page and you'll find an appendix full of useful prompt templates you can use as the basis for your own prompts going forward. I hope you get good use out of them!

# Appendix A

# PROMPT TEMPLATES

Want a head start on your prompt engineering? Here's a set of flexible prompt templates you can adapt across different scenarios, organized by category. Use them as you see fit, substituting your own information for the elements inside the brackets.

# Art and Design Prompts

Analyze the attached image file(s) and generate appropriate brand design guidelines.

Create a design concept for [specific project] incorporating [key elements] and [design principles].

Describe a color scheme and typography set for a [brand style/website type].

Generate 5 creative concepts for a logo for [business/organization].

Provide inspiration and ideas for [creative project] drawing from [specific themes] and [artistic styles].

Suggest 10 visual metaphors for representing [abstract concept].

Write a creative brief for a designer to create [ad/banner/flyer] for [audience].

Write a critique of [artwork] analyzing its [composition], [color palette], and [emotional impact].

# Brainstorming Prompts

Brainstorm [number] ideas for [topic]. The ideas should be [describe desired qualities].

Combine [concept A] with [concept B] to create a new idea.

Generate 10 creative uses for [object/technology].

Generate ideas for [project/task] considering [specific parameters].

Suggest improvements to [product/service/idea].

What are some out-of-the-box ways to solve [problem]?

# Business-Related Prompts

Conduct market research on [specific industry] identifying [trends], [opportunities], and [challenges].

Create a business plan for a [type of business] targeting [specific market].

Create a persuasive pitch deck outline for [idea/product].

Develop a leadership development plan for [specific role] focusing on [key skills] and [leadership style].

Provide advice for launching a startup in [specific industry], including [key steps] and [common pitfalls].

Summarize the attached business report into key takeaways for an executive audience.

Write a LinkedIn post introducing [product/idea], highlighting [benefit].

# Conversational Prompts

Ask me about my day like you're a curious coworker during a coffee break.

Chat with me like a friend texting me at the end of the day. What would you say?

Generate a list of conversation starters for a [specific occasion/event].

Let's have a laid-back chat. What's something simple that made you smile today?

Let's play a quick word association game. Give me a word, and I'll respond with the first thing that comes to mind.

Let's discuss [topic] and share our thoughts and opinions.

Pretend you're my neighbor catching me outside. What's the casual small talk you'd start with?

Start a casual conversation with me, like we just bumped into each other at the grocery store.

# Critical Thinking Prompts

Argue for/against [ethical issue] considering [different perspectives] and [moral implications].

Compare how [two cultures/systems] approach [issue].

Explore the implications of [philosophical concept] on [specific aspect of life].

List 3 counterarguments to the claim [statement].

Prepare arguments for and against [topic] to help me prepare for a debate.

# Cross-Cultural Prompts

Compare how [holiday/custom] is celebrated in [country A] vs. [country B].

Explain how [global event] affected [country/region].

Summarize cultural dos and don'ts when doing business in [region].

Translate [concept] into culturally relevant terms for [audience].

What lessons can [culture/region] teach us about [topic]?

# Education and Learning Prompts

Create a quiz for [audience] with [X] multiple-choice questions on [topic].

Create an interactive classroom activity for teaching [topic] to [audience].

Design a course outline for [subject], covering [key topics] and [learning objectives].

Design a short lesson plan for teaching [topic] to [audience].

Draft a training module outline for [skill/job role].

Explain [complex concept] in simple terms, suitable for a [grade level] student.

Explain [concept] using the Socratic method.

Generate a study guide for [exam/subject] covering key concepts and questions.

Provide study tips and strategies for improving [specific academic skill] and achieving [academic goal].

Recommend online resources for learning [specific skill/subject] including [tutorials], [videos], and [interactive tools].

Summarize [complex idea] in increasing levels of detail: 1 sentence, 1 paragraph, 1 page.

Write 10 flashcards for memorizing [subject matter].

# Emotional Support Prompts

[Event] just happened. Help me deal with my [emotions] about what happened.

Help me reflect on my thoughts and feelings about [topic/experience].

Offer words of comfort and support for someone dealing with [emotional challenge].

Provide guidance on how to navigate a difficult situation involving [issue].

# Finance and Investing Prompts

Compare investment options: [stocks/bonds/real estate/etc.].

Develop a comprehensive financial plan for [specific life event] incorporating [savings], [investments], and [insurance].

Explain how [financial concept] works using a real-world analogy.

Forecast possible scenarios if [economic event] happens.

Give me some budgeting advice for someone earning [amount].

Help me create a budget plan for [specific financial goal] considering [income] and [expenses].

Provide investment advice for [specific financial goal], including [risk tolerance] and [timeframe].

Summarize the impact of [policy/economic trend] on [group/market].

# Food and Cooking Prompts

All I have in my fridge are leftovers: [list leftovers]. Give me some ideas for a quick dinner incorporating only these items.

Create a recipe for [dish] for [number] people, incorporating [specific ingredients] and [cooking methods].

Offer cooking tips and techniques for preparing [specific ingredient] to enhance its flavor and texture.

Plan a [type of] meal for [number] people. The guests like/dislike [specific foods or cuisines].

Suggest a weekly meal plan for someone who [criteria].

Write a review of [restaurant name] highlighting its [atmosphere], [service], and [food quality].

# Health and Wellness Prompts

Compare holistic vs. conventional approaches to [health issue].

Create a patient handout on [topic] that's easy to understand.

Create a workout routine for [fitness goal], incorporating [specific exercises] and [training frequency].

Develop a meal plan for [dietary requirement], focusing on [specific nutrients] and [food preferences].

Draft a wellness plan for someone who wants to improve [fitness, sleep, stress].

Explain [medical condition] in plain language for a patient who has just been diagnosed.

I'm experiencing [symptoms]. Give me a bullet list of questions to ask my physician.

I'm experiencing [symptoms]. What do you think the problem may be?

List common treatment options for [condition], including benefits and side effects.

Offer support and resources for managing [mental health condition], including [coping strategies] and [professional help].

# Humor and Joke Prompts

Give me a five-minute standup routine about [topic] in the style of [comedian].

Playfully tease me about [topic/subject].

Respond to the statement "[statement]" with a healthy dose of sarcasm.

Tell a joke about [topic] that is suitable for [grade level] kids.

Tell me a joke about [topic].

# Image Generation Prompts

Clean up the photo in the attached file. Remove dirt and scratches and make it look like it was recently taken.

Colorize the attached black-and-white image.

Create a [style] depiction of [scene]. Include [specific details]. The atmosphere should feel [mood], with a focus on [elements].

Create an illustration of [character/scene] from [story/genre], with [visual details like clothing, props, mood], in the style of [illustration style/artist].

Generate a [image type] about a [subject] with in the [style] style. The mood should be [mood].

Generate a [image type] in the style of [style/artist], featuring [subject]. Include the following [color/detail].

Generate a [image type] of a [character type/persona] wearing [clothing/accessories], with [expression/pose/gesture], set in [background/environment], in [art style/photography style]

Generate a [image type] of a [natural landscape/environment] during [time of day/season], with [key features like weather, flora, fauna], in the style of [art style/photography style].

Generate a candid photo of [person/character] [doing activity], in [environment/setting], with [lighting/season/time of day], shot in [photography style].

Generate a photo of a [model/person/character] wearing [clothing/accessories], posed in [environment], styled with [fashion/makeup/hair details], shot in [photography/editorial style].

Generate a photo of a [product/object] designed with [materials/colors/textures], displayed on [background/surface], in the style of [photography/rendering technique].

Generate a photographic portrait of [person/character] with [expression/pose], lit by [lighting type].

# Information-Seeking Prompts

Compare [topic A] and [topic B] in terms of [criteria].

Compare and contrast [two or more concepts/objects], highlighting their key differences.

Explain [concept] as if you're teaching it to [audience].

Explain the term [term] and provide examples of its usage.

Give me a step-by-step explanation of how [process] works.

Provide step-by-step instructions for [task/process].

Summarize [article/text/topic] in [X] sentences, highlighting the most important points.

What are the pros and cons of [decision/topic]?

# Job-Hunting and Employment Prompts

Analyze my resume in the attached file and punch it up so that it's appropriate for a [position] position for [company] in [industry].

Conduct a mock interview for a [job title] position, asking relevant questions and providing feedback.

Generate a list of [number] interview questions for a [job title]. The questions should be designed to assess the candidate's [skills]. Include a mix of behavioral and situational questions.

Help me write a professional summary for my resume, highlighting my experience in [field/industry].

Write a cover letter for a [job title] position at [company], showcasing my skills in [specific areas].

# Legal and Compliance Prompts

Simplify this legal agreement into plain-language bullet points for easier client understanding.

Check this contract for redundancy and propose streamlined wording without losing meaning.

Compare how [two jurisdictions] regulate [topic].

Create a compliance checklist for [industry requirement].

Create a sample clause that protects [party A] in case [specific risk] occurs.

Draft a [type of contract, e.g., service agreement, NDA, employment contract] between [party A] and [party B], including sections on [payment terms, confidentiality, termination, and so on].

Draft a sample contract clause for [situation].

Draft a short addendum to this contract allowing for [change].

Explain the legal risks of [decision/scenario].

Outline the standard elements of a legally binding contract under [jurisdiction].

Review the attached contract and suggest additional clauses that should be included in a [type of contract] to protect [party A].

Review the attached contract for potential risks or vague terms. Highlight any clauses that could cause problems for [party A].

Rewrite this contract clause in clearer, more concise legal language while keeping it enforceable.

Suggest dispute resolution mechanisms that could be added to this agreement, with pros and cons for each.

Summarize [law/regulation] in simple, nonlegal terms.

Summarize the key points and obligations of this contract in plain English so a nonlawyer can understand it.

What are the most common legal pitfalls in [industry] contracts, and how can they be avoided?

# Management-Related Prompts

Draft 3 versions of constructive feedback for [scenario].

Outline a performance improvement plan for an underperforming team member.

Suggest strategies for resolving a conflict between [employee A] and [employee B].

Suggest strategies for resolving a conflict between [employee A] and [employee B].

Summarize best practices for leading a remote team.

Write a motivational speech to a team facing [challenge].

# Marketing and Sales Prompts

Create a content calendar with 10 social media post ideas for [platform] about [topic].

Create a social media post for [platform] promoting [product/service] and engaging [target audience].

Develop a sales pitch for [product/service] that addresses [customer pain points] and showcases [unique selling points].

Draft a press release announcing [event/product/service]. Include the following details: [details].

Explain how to position [brand/product] in a crowded market.

Generate 3 different ad copy variations for [product/service].

Suggest 10 blog post ideas for a company in [industry].

Write 5 catchy headlines for an article about [topic].

Write a compelling product description for [product name], highlighting its features and benefits.

# Music Generation Prompts

Create a [genre] track featuring [instruments], with a [mood/feeling], at [tempo/bpm], in the style of [artist/era].

Create a cinematic score using [instruments/sections], evoking [emotion/mood], structured as [scene type], inspired by [composer/film style].

Create an [electronic/ambient] track with [synth/texture elements], evolving over [duration], with a [mood/atmosphere], produced in [style/era].

Create an uptempo [length]-second advertising jingle for a [product/client]. Include the catchphrase, "[catchphrase]."

Generate a [tempo/bpm] [genre] beat with [drum style/percussion instruments], layered with [bass/synth/texture], creating a [mood].

Generate a fusion track blending [cultural style/region] instruments with [modern/traditional] elements, creating a [mood/energy level].

Write a [genre] song with [male/female/choir] vocals, about [theme/subject], with [instrumental backing], in the style of [artist/era].

# Personal Growth Prompts

Give me motivational advice framed as if from [historical figure/coach/friend].

Guide me through a mindfulness exercise to help me relax and focus.

Help me set realistic goals for [area of life] and create an action plan to achieve them.

List practical ways to reduce stress when dealing with [situation].

Provide some tips and strategies for improving [specific skill/habit].

What are 3 small habits that would improve [area of life]?

Write a daily journal entry reflecting on [theme or event].

# Problem-Solving Prompts

Analyze [data/topic/problem] and identify potential risks.

Break down [challenge] into smaller steps and recommend an action plan.

Explain how [decision] might impact [group/market/individual] in the short and long term.

Generate a decision matrix for choosing between [options].

Identify common mistakes people make when dealing with [topic] and how to avoid them.

Identify stakeholders affected by [decision].

I'm having trouble with [issue]. Can you help me identify the cause and potential solutions?

List possible root causes of [problem].

Suggest short-term vs. long-term fixes for [issue].

What are 3 possible solutions to [problem], ranked by feasibility?

# Prompt-Related Prompts

Break down this complex prompt into smaller, more focused prompts: [prompt].

Evaluate this prompt for clarity, bias, and ambiguity: [prompt].

Improve this prompt to get a more creative/detailed response: [prompt].

Suggest 5 variations of a prompt to generate [type of output].

Turn this messy idea into a clear, well-structured prompt: [raw idea].

# Research and Analysis Prompts

Compare how different experts define [concept].

Explain [trend/data] and predict possible future developments.

Give me a timeline of major events in [topic].

Summarize key findings from recent research on [subject].

What gaps exist in current knowledge about [topic]?

# Role-Based Prompts

Act as if you're a [role] and help me with [issue/task].

Explain [topic] as if you're a [role].

Tell me a story about [theme/topic] from the perspective of [character/object].

You are a [role]. Your task is to [task]. The audience is [audience], and the tone should be [tone].

# Speculative Prompts

Describe how [emerging technology] could change [industry/life aspect].

Imagine what daily life might look like in [year].

Predict the next big innovation in [field].

What ethical dilemmas might arise if [sci-fi scenario] became reality?

Write a news article from the year [future date] about [event].

# Technology Prompts

Analyze the best [products] for [use type] and recommend the top three options, with pros and cons for each

Analyze the latest developments in [tech industry] and their potential impact on [specific area].

Design a mobile app for [specific purpose] incorporating [key features] and [user experience].

Explain [technical concept] in detail, including its applications and limitations.

Explain this code snippet step by step: [paste code].

Help me connect [components] in my system.

Help me troubleshoot an issue with [technical product/system] and provide potential solutions.

Offer tips and best practices for protecting [specific device/system] from [cybersecurity threats].

Refactor this code to make it cleaner and more efficient: [paste code].

Write a [Python/Java/JavaScript/and so on] script that does [task].

# Travel and Leisure Prompts

Plan a [length of trip] trip to [destination] including [specific activities] and [accommodation preferences].

Plan a 3-day itinerary for a trip to [destination].

Provide cultural insights and tips for travelers visiting [destination] to help them navigate local customs.

Recommend [number] must-see attractions in [city/destination] for [type of traveler].

We like [previous destinations/activities]. Where would be another vacation destination we might like?

What are the best [price range] hotels in [destination]?

Where should I go on my next vacation? My spouse and I like [activities] and we have a [time frame] available. Our budget is in the [amount] range.

# Video Generation Prompts

Create a [length] music video of [artist/band/character] performing [song/music] in [setting], filmed with [camera angle/movement], featuring [lighting, visual effects, choreography], in the style of [music video style/director].

Create a short portrait-orientation video for social media with [person/character/object] [performing action or challenge] in [setting], with [music or sound effect], designed to be [funny, shocking, satisfying, inspirational].

Create a storyboard outline for a short video about [topic].

Generate a [length] video demonstrating [subject/product/concept], with [camera angle], [text overlays/animations], [background music/mood], in [style].

Generate a [length] video of a [natural/city/environment] scene, showing [change over time/weather/season], shot in [time-lapse/motion style], with [lighting/color palette/mood].

Generate a [length] video where a [subject/character] is [performing action] in [environment/location], shot with [camera angle/type/lens], with [lighting/mood/effects], in the style of [film/director/genre].

Generate a before/after video of [object/person/space] transforming from [before state] to [after state], with [effects/transitions], synced to [music beat/tempo].

Generate a short video showing a [process/action/visual] repeated in a satisfying way, filmed with [angle/movement], featuring [effects, slow-motion, close-ups], designed to loop seamlessly and captivate viewers.

# Writing Prompts

Create a character profile for [character name] including their backstory, motivations, and personality traits.

Draft an email to [audience] about [topic], keeping the tone [tone].

Generate 5 different opening lines for a [type of output] about [topic].

Generate a plot twist for a story about [topic] that adds a surprising layer of complexity.

Outline a three-act structure for a story about [situation].

Reimagine [classic story/event] in a modern-day setting.

Write a [genre] story where [character/situation] happens, but with a surprising twist.

Write a [length] speech for [occasion]. The primary message should be [main message]. The tone should be [tone]. Include a call to action or a memorable closing line.

Write a [type of output] to [person] about [topic]. It should be [length] in a [style] style. Mention the following topic(s): [topics].

Write a [type of writing] about [topic/theme] in the style of [author/genre].

Write a blog post titled "[title of blog post]." The main points to cover are [list key points or subheadings]. The target audience is [audience]. The tone should be [tone]. The length should be [number of words].

Write dialogue between [character A] and [character B] in a situation where [conflict].

# Index

# T